MINDFUL SPICED CHI

G. Kathuria Kelley

Raindrop Publishers
Calgary

A collection of traditional and fusion Chicken recipes from the Modern Indian Kitchen

First Edition

Published in 2012 by Raindrop Publishers, Calgary, Alberta, Canada

Printed in Canada

Mindfully Spiced Chicken Copyright © 2012 by Raindrop Publishers. All rights reserved.

Printed in Canada. No part of this book may be used or reproduced in any manner whatsoever, stored in a retrieval system or transmitted in any form or by any means, electronic, mechanical, photocopying, recording or otherwise without the prior written permission of the publishers and copyright holders.

For information, contact Raindrop Publishers at Suite #326, 370, 5222-130th Avenue SE Calgary AB T2Z 0G4.

All photography Copyright © 2012 by Raindrop Publishers.

Photographs were taken by Lisa Knapik

except for the pictures on Pages 13 and 14 which were taken by G. Kathuria Kelley

Raindrop Publishers books may be purchased for educational, business or sales promotional use. For information, please write: Raindrop Publishers Suite #326, 370, 5222-130th Avenue SE Calgary AB T2Z 0G4. Tel: 403 279 2827

I S B N: 978-0-9867608-08 (Softcover) Canada
978-1480146891 (Softcover) US

Book Cover design by G. K. Kelley

*To my loving grandma who handed me my first pen and paper;
she introduced me to the wonderful world of books*

*To my late grandad who instilled the love of butter chicken in me,
taught me it was important to love food and
life was too short to compromise on the quality and taste of food*

*To my husband Dal and my gorgeous son Jakey who bravely tasted all my
concoctions and enjoyed the recipe tasting*

*To my loving parents,
and especially my mum for always being there
whenever I needed anything, and for
guiding me through difficult times*

*To my beautiful sister Julie, my brother in law Raj and
my gorgeous niece Serena for all their love and support*

*To all my family and friends for encouraging me to cook
and for their constant love and support;
without them, I simply would not exist*

I would like to thank the following:

Crossroads Farmers Market, Calgary
Cristian Bancos and friends at Crown Prosecutions Office, Calgary
Mann Law, Mississauga especially Mr Harry Mann and Harjaap Mann
Paola Kathuria
Marco Kathuria
Sylvia Spruck Wrigley
Darlene and Dave Hetherington
Vanessa and Anthony Canevaro
Rebcecca Fong at Le Creuset, Calgary
Amanda Keip at PC Cooking School, Calgary
Lisa Knapik for her beautiful photographs

CONTENTS

INTRODUCTION

SOUPS AND SALADS

KEBABS AND APPETISERS

WINGS AND DRUMMETTES

TRADITIONAL CHICKEN

NON-TRADITIONAL CHICKEN

CHUTNEYS AND SPICES

INDEX

Introduction

I have to confess that I didn't really know how to cook until I was about 28 years old. I could manage the normal things like Beans on toast, Salads, Dips and Sandwiches but not a lot more than that. My gran had handed me my pens and paper when I was about a year old. My love for books, reading and writing started at a very early age thanks to my gran and I couldn't wait to start School.

However, my late grandfather instilled the love of food in me. I believe he was the original foodie, well before the name foodie was discovered. He brought his love for good food with him when he came from Pakistan to India and that love developed into a hobby as he got older. I have memories of him taking us to the original Moti Mahal restaurant in old Delhi, and whilst I did not remember the name I remembered the food and the dressed up security guard who welcomed us in. He taught us that it was the real butter chicken that reminded him of his home in Pakistan, and there was nothing like it anywhere. Little did he know that he was right.

My grandad had to have butter chicken at least once a week from Moti Mahal in Old Delhi, and if he had company it would have been delivered again. Chicken Tikka and Butter Chicken from Moti Mahal were his favourites, and he had specific places for specific foods he liked. I was fortunate that I got to go to many places with him, and taste all kinds of foods as a child. I retravelled and visited all these destinations when I returned to India in 2006.

I have never had the time for cooking, although I appreciated good food and was a fussy eater! I still have nostalgic memories of going to street vendors with my young Uncles and Aunts every evening when I was in India. Whilst I watched everyone cook, I didn't have the desire to cook. I have fantastic memories of watching my gran make the most delectable food with tons of love in every morsel she fed me. I also watched one of my Aunts, who is an amazing cook and her ability to make trillions of different recipes always fascinated me.

As a teenager I started cutting out recipes and writing recipes in my journals. I have no explanation as to what I thought I was going to do with them, but my scrap book collection on recipes has grown over the years and this habit continues till today.

It wasn't until I was 28 and had moved into my own place all by myself that I had the opportunity of buying groceries and cooking by myself. Supermarket shopping fascinated me to no end, and I remember shopping at Tesco's in the middle of the night just to be able to have lots of time to peruse through and check all the new ingredients, sauces and spices. It became my form of retail therapy after a stressful day at work, but it led to the added problem of having way too much food in the pantry and fridge. Hence, began my search for volunteers to feed my new concoctions. I couldn't let good food go to waste, but I was fortunate enough to have a stream of friends who happily volunteered to test my concoctions.

My passion for cooking grew and so did my abundant collection of cook books, sauce mixes, spice rubs and other pantry ingredients. Finally, after my husband moved in with me, we started the trend of travelling a different country every weekend. This was my opportunity to cook breakfast, lunch and dinner from a cook book from that country. So we had Mexican weekends, Italian weekends, Indian weekends, British weekends and so on. It was a lot of fun and the only problem was, I didn't get the chance to repeat any of our favourite recipes. I was lucky to have had an abundance of volunteers though.

In 2006 I travelled back to India after a very long time and this time, I took notes of how things were actually being cooked. I was fascinated to see how food tasted so different in India and how we could never bring the same flavour into our food at home. Learning different ways of roasting spices and how different ways of applying them to our cooking affected the flavours became one of my pet interests as well as art of balancing spices.

One thing led to another and cooking became my life and passion. This book has taken me over 3 years to put together as I got more interested in cooking and experimenting with food than with the writing process. I am so very grateful to God for giving me the opportunity of getting this book out eventually, and I know my Gran will be very happy. She predicted many years ago that I will write books, and I know she'll be extremely proud to see this book.

In this book, I have tried to put together all my favourite Chicken recipes as well as the family favourites. There are some traditional restaurant style dishes as well as some modern dishes, but these are modified and cooked my way. I like to keep cooking simple without too many frills, and without an unnecessary use of spices. I like to be able to taste my food and use spices for flavour enhancement, texture, medicinal purpose or as a preservative.

Whilst I love slow cooking, realistically not many people have the time or the desire to spend long hours in the kitchen. I have used normal every day spices in most recipes, that are readily available in the shops now. I have deliberately not used many whole spices, as the children and men in our family spend way too much time picking them out of their food and complaining about the 'spice things'. I simply grind them to a powder or paste, so as to get the flavour into the food and to keep their fishing spoons at bay.

I love the delicate flavour of spices when it accentuates the flavour of food instead of the overpowering strong flavours that sometimes take over the dish. However, there are some dishes that absolutely need that little flavour boost. The recipes in this book range from lightly flavoured to strongly flavoured Chicken dishes, as well as a fusion of flavours and traditional flavours.

Whilst some of my friends out there would probably appreciate more chilli being added to the recipes, so I have made these recipes adaptable to enable my friends to add their extra chillies where necessary. I wanted to carry on writing more chicken recipes as I can still think of another couple of dozen to add to the book, but it was high time to get the book printed after 4 years so I am just sticking to my favourite recipes in this book.

I have had a lot of fun putting this set of recipes together and I hope you get as much enjoyment from reading this book, cooking these recipes and of course, sharing them with your friends and family.

Ginni Kathuria Kelley

Introduction to the Modern Indian Kitchen

In the vanguard of the Nouvelle Indian Kitchen, these recipes started with a simple idea of juxtaposing some modern and inventive takes on Indian cuisine. Whilst there is an array of traditional authentic recipes in the book, the belief that any food can be thoughtfully spiced and seasoned with Indian flavours to create a familiar, yet inspired variety of dishes remains strong throughout this book. From delicately spiced salads and soups to strongly flavoured Vindaloos and Kormas, there are recipes to suit all spice palates.

The traditional recipes are made with a lot of extra love and indulgence, in the form of butter and cream whilst the contemporary ones are somewhat lighter and healthier. There's a variety of chicken dinners and snack ideas, drawing inspiration from all over the world.

My New Indian Kitchen uses boneless and skinless chicken breasts for most of the chicken recipes, and is flexible on heat. The spiceometer is controlled by your own capacity to handle heat and most of the dishes can be enjoyed by children if you leave the green chillies out.

The spices are ground and not whole for ease of convenience, even though I grind mine from scratch I see no shame in using ready mix blends to save time on a daily basis. I have not overloaded dishes with a load of preservative spices and I am a firm believer that simple cooking process works every time. My freezer is my best friend and I love using the freezer to save me time in creating lots of different dishes.

Spices

I have used normal every day spices in most of the recipes but there are bound to be some ingredients that may not be as easy to find, without a trip to the Indian grocery store. I usually make one trip to the Indian grocery store which is about a 45 minutes drive for me, and stock up on spices, fresh coriander leaves (that I chop and freeze), green chillies (just wash and freeze), ginger (wash and freeze), garlic (its ready peeled in a large jar that goes into the refrigerator). This supply usually keeps me going for a couple of months at least.

For the spices, I keep a supply of garam masala (readily available, but can be easily made at home), chicken masala (recipe in this book) and chaat masala (readily available). If I get the ready made ones, I get the smaller boxed containers, as they don't last very long and get used quite quickly.

Once every six months I make a huge purchase of whole spices and roast all the spices. However, I grind them in small batches as I use them.

A couple of recipes ask for specific methods of roasting and grinding spices, and these are addressed individually with the recipe.

Measurements

When I started reading old Indian cookbooks and recipes, I always found that there was something wrong with some of the spice measurements and until you adjusted them, they didn't taste right. The same thing happened when I was watching some Indian TV Shows and the penny dropped when I was observing my Aunt in India cooking. I asked her what she meant by a teaspoon and her teaspoon was way tinier than the teaspoon that we use. Then I looked at the table spoon size, and the cup measurements she used, they were all so very different.

So, I wanted to clarify the size of the spoons and measurements that I have used. I have used the standard US spoon and cup measurements which amount to the following measurements:-

1 tsp	5 ml
1 tbsp	15 ml
1 cup	240ml
2 cups (1 pint)	470ml
4 cups (1 quart)	.95 litre
4 quarts (1 gallon)	3.8 litres

I am also including a short temperature conversion chart:

Celsius	Fahrenheit	Gas Mark	Description
300	150	2	Slow
325	160/170	3	Moderate
350	180	4	Moderate
375	190	5	Moderately Hot
400	200	6	Moderately Hot
425	220	7	Hot

Serving Size
All the recipes comfortably serve 4 adults as a minimum.

Soups and Salads

Chicken Mulligatawny Soup
Chicken and Tomato Soup
Chicken and Mushroom Soup
Dal's Hot and Sour Chicken Soup
Mango Chicken Salad
Spiced Coronation Chicken Salad
Arabic Chicken & Peach Salad
Spiced Orange & Chicken Salad
Thai Coconut Chicken Soup
Tikka Salad

Chicken Mulligatawny Soup

Chicken Mulligatawny Soup
A warm and comforting soup, softly spiced and beautifully flavoured

Ingredients:
2 small onions, finely chopped
2 stalks of celery, finely chopped
2 medium size carrots, finely chopped
1 cup red lentils
1 can crushed tomatoes or 4 whole tomatoes
1 inch piece of ginger, cut into thin julienne strips
4 cloves of garlic, crushed and finely chopped
2 chicken breasts (350gms)
juice and zest of one lemon
1 inch piece of cinnamon bark
1 fresh green chilli (optional), finely chopped
3 tsp cumin coriander powder
2 tsp black pepper
2 tsp turmeric powder
5 tsp curry powder
3 tbsp oil
salt to taste
¼ cup heavy / full fat cream (optional)

Preparation:
Boil the chicken breasts using 6 cups of water, and place the cinnamon bark in the water. Reserve the water, and shred the chicken into bite size chunks. Remove the cinnamon bark and discard.
Wash the lentils under running water, until water runs clear of the starch.
If using whole tomatoes then puree using a hand blender, or a food processor.

Method:
In a large pot heat the oil and add the finely chopped onions for 3-4 minutes. Saute until the onions soften and turn translucent in colour. Add the ginger, green chillies, celery, carrots and the garlic. Continue cooking for 3-4 minutes stirring occasionally.

Add the spices, and the lemon zest. Stir them in and mix thoroughly before adding the tomatoes.
Add the lentils and the reserved water from the boiled chicken. You can use chicken stock instead of this reserved water if you prefer.

Stir and lower the heat to low-medium. Cover the pot and let this cook for 20-25 minutes. You may need to add more water, so best to check half way through and add more water if necessary. If you prefer a smooth soup, now is the time to use a hand blender in the soup, before adding the chicken.

Add the chicken to the soup, stir and let it simmer for a further 20 minutes, if the soup looks too thick, you may add more water or chicken stock. Stir in the lemon juice and the fresh cilantro and the soup is ready to be served.

Variation:
Heat some oil or clarified butter in a small pan, add half a tsp. of mustard seeds, some chilli flakes or finely chopped green chilli. Let the mustard seeds pop in the hot oil and pour this sizzling ghee over the soup along with a spoonful of heavy cream for the added love in the soup.

Chicken And Tomato Soup

A 'feel good' soup that I learnt from my youngest Uncle. He makes a guest appearance in the kitchen once every 10 years but anything he cooks is always memorable!
I have added some additional ingredients to the original version of soup my Uncle made, but its still heart-warming and comforting. It cures my winter cold, every time.

Ingredients:
1 medium size onion, finely chopped
2 medium size potatoes, cut into ½ inch cubes
2 boneless, skinless chicken breasts (350gms), cut into ½ inch cubes
2 sticks of celery, finely chopped
2 cloves of garlic, minced
2 inch piece of ginger, grated
6 medium size plum tomatoes - (equivalent to 1.5 cans)
1 green chilli (optional), deseeded and finely chopped
½ tsp freshly ground black pepper
3 tbsp oil
1 tsp cumin seeds
¼ tsp fennel powder
¼ cup fresh coriander (including stems), finely chopped
4 cups / 900 ml chicken stock
3 stalks of green onion / spring onion, finely chopped
½ tsp garam masala
1 tsp coriander powder
½ tsp lemon juice
salt to taste

Preparation:
Boil some water in a large pot, blanch the tomatoes in there for a minute before transferring them into a bowl full of ice water. This helps remove the skins off the tomatoes. Once the tomatoes are peeled, cut them into small cubes.

Method:
Heat oil in a large pot. Saute the onions, the ginger and the celery, until they soften and the onions are a soft golden in colour. Add the tomatoes and the garlic, and continue cooking for a further 3-4 minutes. Taking a hand blender, blitz the onion tomato mixture to a smooth thick paste.

Add the potatoes and the chicken stock to the soup, along with all the spices and the chicken cubes. Cook in a covered pot for 20-25 minutes.

Sprinkle some freshly chopped coriander on top before serving. Serve with a slice of freshly toasted garlic bread and a dollop of heavy cream for extra love.

Chicken and Mushroom Soup

This is one of my husbands favourites, and he likes his soup with the extra spice and cream. Its a super easy and quick soup, thats also perfect for when you have company.

Ingredients:
2 boneless, skinless chicken breasts (350gms)
8-10 pieces button mushrooms, thinly sliced
1 medium size onion, finely chopped
1 green chilli, finely chopped
2 cups chicken stock
¼ tsp lemon juice
½ tsp sugar
1 tsp cumin coriander powder
1 tsp freshly ground black pepper
2 tbsp oil
salt to taste

For garnish:
fresh coriander leaves for garnishing
¼ cup heavy cream (optional)

Method:
Heat oil in a large pot. Saute the onions and the green chilli until the onions are soft and translucent in colour. Add all the remaining ingredients into the soup, along with the whole chicken breasts. Cover and let this simmer until the chicken is fully cooked. Remove the chicken, shred and keep aside.

Taking a hand blender, blitz the soup until its smooth. Add the shredded chicken back into the soup and stir in the cream. Sprinkle some finely chopped fresh coriander leaves on top and serve with your favourite crackers or buttered bread.

Dal's Hot and Sour Chicken Soup

My husband's ultimate winter time soup that he can have for dinner, everyday, without a complaint, especially when he has a cold.

Ingredients:
1 boneless, skinless chicken breast cut into thin strips
1 large egg, lightly beaten
2 inch piece firm tofu (or bean curd if available), cut into tiny cubes
1 cup prawns / shrimp (uncooked)
4 cups / 900 ml chicken stock
½ cup fresh bean sprouts
2 green chillies, finely chopped
3 inch piece ginger, grated
½ cup ketchup
½ cup white vinegar
1 tsp white pepper
2 tbsp corn flour
1 tsp sugar
1 tsp chilli sauce
3 tbsp dark soya sauce
1 tbsp worcestershire sauce
½ cup shredded cabbage
3 medium sized carrots, finely chopped or grated
fresh coriander, finely chopped
salt to taste

Method:
Make a corn flour paste using 6 tbsp of water. Marinate the chicken with half of the corn flour paste for at least 25 minutes. Put the stock to boil in a large pot. As it reaches boiling point and starts to bubble add the marinated chicken.

Let the chicken cook for about 5 minutes, on medium low heat. Stir in the tofu, the carrots, the cabbage and the bean sprouts. Reduce the heat to a low, and cover the pot. Allow to simmer for 10-15 minutes until the chicken is fully cooked and the vegetables have softened.

Save the egg and the vinegar, and add all the remaining ingredients into the soup, including the reserved corn flour paste. Allow to simmer for a couple of minutes before stirring in the beaten egg, a tablespoon at a time and remove from heat. Stir in the vinegar. If the soup is too runny, add some more corn flour paste, made using a tsp of corn flour and cold water.

Sprinkle some fresh coriander as a garnish before serving.

Variation:
Fried noodles and fried ginger strips make this soup extra special, especially when you have company. I like to use them as a garnish that looks like a little nest on top of the soup.

Mango Chicken Salad
Delicious spicy sweet and refreshing flavours, wonderful for a Summer BBQ

Ingredients:
2 mangoes, peeled and cut into small cubes
4 boneless, skinless chicken breasts (700gms)
2 cloves garlic, crushed and finely minced
1 red pepper/capsicum, sliced
2 green pepper/capsicum, sliced
1 small red onion, finely sliced
1 inch piece of ginger, grated
½ tsp red chilli flakes (optional)
1 tbsp chicken masala
1 tsp chaat masala
1 fresh lime
1 tbsp pomegranate seeds
Mixed green salad or lettuce of your choice
1 fresh red chilli, finely chopped (optional)

Dressing:
1 tsp olive oil
2 tbsp mango chutney
1 tsp cumin coriander powder
½ tsp chaat masala
1 tsp honey
½ tsp red chilli powder (optional)
1/3 greek yogurt

Method:
Preheat oven to 375F / 190C / Gas Mark 5. Make a couple of slits in the thickest part of the chicken. Rub some of the minced garlic onto the chicken and into the slits. Combine the chaat masala and the chicken masala, with some salt and pepper and rub onto the chicken. Spray a little oil on the chicken and place on a lightly greased baking sheet. Roast in oven for 15-20 minutes or until cooked through.

In the meantime, combine all the dressing ingredients in a small jar and set aside until ready to use.
Dry roast the pomegranate seeds on a skillet and set aside.

Using ½ a tsp of oil in a pan, saute the ginger and add the peppers and onions. As soon as they soften a little remove from heat, as you don't want them to lose their shape and crunchiness. Season with a little salt and freshly ground black pepper.

In a plate, spread the lettuce and/or salad greens to make a base. Next spread some of the peppers and onions. Slice the chicken and add to the plate, followed by the mango cubes. Sprinkle some pomegranate seeds, some lime zest and lime juice, before drizzling the dressing.

Spiced Coronation Chicken Salad
Traditional British Coronation Chicken Salad spiced up with Indian flavours

Ingredients:
2 boneless, skinless chicken breasts (350gms), boiled, cooled and cubed
2 shallots, finely chopped
1 tbsp tomato puree / tomato paste
1 tbsp curry powder
1 tsp cumin coriander powder
¼ tsp freshly ground black pepper
2 tbsp apricot jam
4 tbsp mayonnaise
4 tbsp thick greek yogurt
4 tbsp sour cream
1 tbsp lemon juice
1 tbsp finely chopped fresh coriander leaves
½ tsp balsamic vinegar
½ tsp worcestershire sauce
1 green chilli, finely chopped
salt to taste

Method:
Heat oil in a skillet. Saute the shallots and green chillies for a couple of minutes. Reduce the heat and add the tomato puree.

Stir in the curry powder and the cumin coriander powder, followed by ½ a cup of water.
Add the worcestershire sauce, salt, pepper and the lemon juice. Cover the pan and continue simmering on low heat for 5-7 minutes until the sauce reduces a bit. Let it cool.

In a bowl, combine all the remaining ingredients and add the chicken. Mix well.

I like to add halved green grapes and roasted almonds to my salad, but that's entirely optional. Serve on a bed of lettuce or spooned in individual lettuce leaves to make lettuce wraps.

Variation:
Try them as sandwiches made using fresh bread rolls and add some watercress salad for an amazing experience.

Arabic Chicken and Peach Salad
There's nothing traditional about this Salad

Ingredients:
4 boneless, skinless chicken breasts
4 cloves garlic, minced
½ cup fresh lemon juice
2 tsp cumin coriander powder
2 tbsp oil
2 tsp cinnamon powder
½ tsp cardamom powder
1 tsp cayenne pepper
½ tsp freshly ground black pepper
Salt to taste

3 ripe peaches, quartered and pitted
2 ears shucked corn, broken into smaller pieces
2 cups Watercress / Baby Spinach Salad

Sauce / Dressing:
2 tbsp Sriracha sauce
1 ½ tbsp honey
1 tbsp olive oil

Method:
Combine all the dry spices, the lemon juice and oil in a ziploc bag. Make a couple of slits on the thickest part of the chicken breast and marinate the chicken in the ziploc bag, in the refrigerator for at least an hour.

Preheat oven to 375F / 190C / Gas Mark 5, place the chicken on a lightly greased baking tray and bake in oven for 15-20 minutes or until the chicken is cooked through.

Grill the corn on a stove top grill or a BBQ for about 5 minutes, until corn is tender. Alternatively, steam cook the corn until tender. Grill the peach quarters or use a stove top griddle to give the peaches some griddle marks, cook for only 1 minute. Keep aside.

Take a large platter. Scatter the watercress or baby spinach all over the base of the platter. Add the griddled corn and peaches. Slice the chicken into smaller pieces and also add to the platter.

Combine the ingredients for the sauce, and drizzle over the salad. Serve with some roasted garlic bread for a lovely Summer lunch.

Spiced Orange and Chicken Salad
My twist on traditional Lebanese Chicken

Ingredients:
2 boneless, skinless chicken breasts (350gms), cut into 1 inch cubes
2 tbsp oil
2 cloves garlic, minced
1 medium size red onion, thinly sliced
zest and juice from one orange
2 medium size oranges
¼ tsp cinnamon
¼ tsp all spice
½ tsp paprika
¼ cup orange juice
baby spinach or any other salad greens of your choice
1 tbsp honey
salt and freshly ground black pepper to taste

Dressing:-
2 tbsp honey
2 tbsp orange juice
salt and freshly ground black pepper to taste
½ tsp cumin coriander powder
½ tsp cayenne pepper (adjust to taste)
1 tbsp olive oil
1 tbsp balsamic vinegar
1 tbsp cornstarch mixed with ½ of the orange juice (optional) to make a thicker dressing

Method:
Heat the oil in a pan and saute half of the onions and the garlic for a couple of minutes until the onions have softened.

Add the chicken and stir fry until there is a light golden coating on the chicken. Stir in some salt, freshly ground black pepper, all spice, cinnamon, paprika, honey, orange juice and the zest. Cover and let it simmer for 15 minutes, until the chicken has cooked through.

Remove the chicken pieces, but leave any sauce still in the pan and stir in all the ingredients for the dressing. If you prefer a thicker dressing like I do, then add some cornstarch mixed with a bit of the orange juice to the dressing.

Serve the chicken on a bed of baby spinach, with the other half of the sliced onions and orange slices. Drizzle the dressing on top.

Thai Coconut Chicken Soup

My son loves this soup, its light, flavourful and delicately spiced.

Ingredients:
1 boneless, skinless chicken breast (175 gms) cut into thin strips
1 can coconut milk
2 tsp sugar
½ tsp salt (adjust to taste)
1 inch piece fresh ginger, cut into thin julienne strips
½ tsp lemon juice
2 bay leaves
1 tsp white pepper
1 tsp oil
2 cups chicken stock, and 2 cups water
½ green pepper (capsicum), finely chopped
1 tsp cumin coriander powder
1 fresh green chilli (optional), finely chopped
A small bunch fresh coriander leaves, finely chopped

Method:
In a large pot, heat the oil and add the julienned ginger strips. Saute the ginger and add the chicken. Let the chicken cook for a couple of minutes before adding in all the remaining ingredients, except the coconut milk and the fresh coriander. Add 2 cups of water and stir the ingredients well.

Cover the pot and lower the heat, allowing the soup to cook for 20 minutes before adding in the coconut milk and the freshly chopped coriander leaves.

Stir the soup well and allow the soup to cook for a further 10 minutes uncovered, on medium heat before serving.

Serve garnished with fried ginger strips and fresh coriander.

Tikka Salad

My twist to the old Chicken Tikka Salad, traditionally served in India to the men when they want to have a wee drink. I like to make this Salad when I am organising a dinner buffet for friends. It does disappear with an amazing speed, and its ever so easy to make.

Ingredients:
Chicken Tikka Boti Kebabs (for recipe see page 29)
2 tbsp mint and coriander chutney (for recipe see page 102)
1 tbsp mango chutney (for recipe see page 102)
1 tsp olive oil

1 cup cherry tomatoes, halved
1 cup shredded iceberg lettuce
1 english cucumber, thinly sliced
1 large red onion, cut into very thin slices
2 lemons
2 tsp chaat masala
a pinch of cayenne pepper
2 green chillies (optional, but good as a garnish)
salt and freshly ground black pepper to taste
a handful of fresh coriander leaves, finely chopped

Method:
Combine the mint chutney, the mango chutney and the olive oil in a small jar, shake and set aside.

To assemble the salad start by sprinkling the lettuce in the centre of a round/oval platter. Taking one slice of cucumber at a time, place them around the edge of the platter letting them overlap a little to make a neat pattern.

If you have any left over cucumber slices, halve them and sprinkle them in the centre. Separate the onion slices and sprinkle these in the centre of the salad platter too.

Depending on the size of the chicken tikka pieces, you may or may not need to halve them. If they are not too big, and are bite size, leave them as they are and place them neatly over the salad platter in the centre. Decorate the cherry tomato halves around them.

Slice one of the lemons, and decorate the slices in the platter. Slit the green chillies lengthways and place these standing, with the slit side up in the platter as a garnish.

Sprinkle chaat masala, cayenne pepper, salt, black pepper all over the salad. Squeeze the juice out of one lemon all over the salad and sprinkle the fresh coriander leaves as a garnish.

Drizzle some of the chutney dressing and serve with some extra mint chutney on the side as a dip, for those who want it extra spicy.

Kebabs and Appetisers

Chapli Kebabs
BBQ Chicken Malai Boti Kebabs
Chicken Tikka Boti Kebabs
Pistachio Chicken Kebabs
Reshmi Kebabs
Chicken Shwarma
Serena's Baked Chicken Strips
Chicken Tikka Turnovers
Dad's Chicken Chaat
Chicken 65
Chicken Shashlik
Chicken Pakoras
Handi Kebab
Tunday Kebabs
Seekh Kebabs
Honey Spiced Chicken Skewers

Chicken Samosas

Chicken Samosas

These samosas taste the best when prepared using ready made samosa pastry sheets, as they turn out a lot more crispier than handmade pastry. The chicken flavour really stands out when the pastry is thin and crispy.

Filling:-
1 lb chicken mince
½ tsp garam masala
1 tsp chicken masala
1 tbsp cumin coriander powder
1 medium onion, finely chopped
2 tbsp oil
1 cup frozen peas
a handful of fresh coriander leaves, finely chopped
½ cup cashew nuts, roughly chopped
salt to taste
2 green chillies, deseeded and finely chopped (adjust to taste)

Samosa pastry strips
Oil for deep frying or baking

Method:
Heat oil in a large pan and saute the onions until soft and translucent in colour. Add the frozen peas and cook on medium heat for 3-4 minutes.

Lower the heat and add the minced chicken to the pan. Use your hands to break up the minced chicken as it will make it easier to cook. Using a wooden spoon, stir the chicken in the pan, breaking up any lumps with the spoon as well as separating the minced chicken. It is imperative to stir well at this point to allow the even cooking of the chicken and to break up any lumps of meat.

Once the chicken is cooked through and the texture feels right and crumbly, add the spices to the chicken and stir in the cashew nut pieces. Sprinkle a few drops of lemon juice or dried mango powder to the chicken filling before removing from heat. Allow the filling to cool down completely to room temperature before making the samosas.

Method of preparing the Samosas:
Prepare and handle the samosa pastry sheets according to the instructions of the packet, as there a large variety of sheets readily available in supermarkets or grocery stores. Make a paste using plain flour and a little bit of water to ensure the samosas are sealed properly.

Deep fry the samosas until they are a crispy golden in colour. Drain excess oil on kitchen paper before serving with fresh mint chutney.

Chapli Kebabs

I love these kebabs and I always keep a supply of these in my freezer for that emergency lunch or snack. They are lovely on their own, or sandwiched in a small burger bun with some spicy chutneys and salad. They are not the most beautiful of kebabs but their flavour makes up for their lack of beauty. The name chapli is derived from the Pashto word 'Chaprikh' which means flat. Their literal translation to English would be flip flop kebabs, which is my favourite word for them. Traditionally these are shallow fried on a skillet, but I bake them in the oven for a more healthier alternative.

Ingredients:
2 lbs boneless minced chicken
4 hard boiled eggs, cooled and finely chopped
2 eggs, lightly whisked
1 tbsp coriander powder
1 tbsp pomegranate powder
1 tbsp red chilli powder
1 tsp cumin powder
1 tsp freshly ground black pepper
½ tsp garam masala
2 green chillies, deseeded and minced
3 tbsp bread crumbs
1 inch piece of fresh ginger, grated
3 cloves of garlic, minced
2 – 3 fresh tomatoes, cut into thin round slices of about half a cm thickness
a handful of fresh coriander leaves, finely chopped
Salt to taste

Method:
Even though we are working with ready minced chicken, for these kebabs we need it minced twice. Ideally you run all the ingredients through a meat grinder (save the boiled eggs and tomatoes) to get a smooth texture.

However, I use a food processor. I grind all the wet ingredients first, then I add the spices and then half the chicken. It gets a bit difficult to run the machine, so I do this in two batches. All the ingredients, save the tomato slices and the boiled eggs should combine fully. Rub some oil in your hands and gently knead the chicken mixture to help smooth out the ingredients. Once its all mixed well, add the chopped boiled eggs, and knead it in well into the chicken mixture. Let the mixture rest for half an hour in the refrigerator.

Heat the oven to 375F / 190C / Gas Mark 5.

Keep a bowl of cold water on one side, as this mixture will be a bit sticky, so you would need to dip your hands in water every time you try to make a patty. Do not use too much water, just wet the hands to prevent the meat sticking. Make flat round or oval patties, using approximately half a cup of the mixture. Press one slice of the tomato onto one side of the patty. Place the patty, tomato side down on a lightly greased baking sheet. Bake for about 10 minutes or until the chicken patties are cooked through.

Since the patties are quite thin, they cook quite quickly. I like to sprinkle my kebabs with a little chaat masala before serving with some mint chutney. These kebabs can be very addictive and they freeze very well.

BBQ Chicken Malai Boti
Melt in your mouth Chicken kebabs marinated in spicy cream

Ingredients:
2 lbs. boneless, skinless chicken, cut into 1 inch cubes
¼ cup greek yogurt
½ cup thick heavy cream
2-3 green chillies (adjust to taste)
½ cup fresh coriander leaves
zest and juice of 1 lemon
1 ½ tbsp cumin coriander powder
1 tsp white pepper powder
1 tsp freshly ground black pepper powder
1 tsp red chilli powder (optional, and adjust to taste)
1 tsp pomegranate seed powder (optional)
1 tsp chicken masala
3 cloves garlic, minced
1 inch piece of ginger
2 tbsp melted butter
1 tbsp cashew nut powder

Method:
Wash the chicken and dry out any excess moisture by using kitchen towels. Spread the chicken on some kitchen towels whilst you prepare the marinade.

In a blender, grind the green chillies, the fresh coriander and the ginger using a bit of the lemon juice. Combine everything in a ziploc bag and mix really well before adding the chicken pieces to this. Let the chicken marinate in this bag for at least 8 hours if not, overnight.

Remove the chicken from the ziploc bag but do not discard the extra marinade. Remove excess marinade from the chicken before threading the chicken onto skewers. Grill the skewers in the BBQ for about 5 minutes on each side. I like to brush them with a little melted butter halfway through the grilling process for extra flavour.

In a small pan, heat up the marinating sauce, to this add some extra cream, a little butter and some ground green chilli and coriander paste. Pour this over the chicken kebabs before serving, on a bed of rice or with some naan bread and salad. This sauce is not traditional and can be omitted, it is just my twist for extra spicy decadence.

Chicken Tikka Boti
Creamy Tandoori flavoured Chicken Tikka bites

Ingredients:
2 lbs. boneless, skinless chicken cut into 1 inch cubes
1 cup yogurt
½ cup heavy cream
2 inch piece of ginger
2 cloves of garlic
½ cup fresh coriander leaves
2-4 green chillies (adjust to taste)
2 fresh lemons + 1 tsp of lemon juice
1 tbsp cumin coriander powder
2 drops of red and 4 drops of yellow food colour (optional)
1 tsp dried fenugreek leaves, crushed betwen the palms of your hands
1 tsp mango powder
1 tsp chicken masala
Salt and freshly ground black pepper to taste

Method:
In a small blender combine the ginger, garlic, coriander leaves, green chillies and a tsp of lemon juice to make a smooth paste.

Combine all the ingredients in a zip loc bag and mix well. Add the chicken and gently massage the chicken from outside to help the marination process. Keep refrigerated for least 6 hours if not overnight. There are many ways to cook the kebabs, on the skillet, shallow fried in a pan, on skewers in the BBQ, a Grill, a hot oven or the tandoor.

I like to spread them out on a lightly greased baking tray that I line with 2 sheets of aluminium foil to help cleaning afterwards, and lighly spray them with oil or you may use butter. Cook them in a hot oven at 375F / 190C / Gas Mark 5 for 15 minutes, turn them over and return to cook for a further 10 minutes or until the chicken has fully cooked through.

Squeeze some lemon juice on top and sprinkle some chaat masala before serving hot with red onion rings. A refreshing cooling mint chutney complements the flavours really well.

Pistachio Chicken Kebabs

These lightly spiced creamy, green coloured nutty Kebabs conjure up memories of sitting by the Thames sipping Pimms and Lemonade. Whilst they are not remotely related, they are perfect for Garden parties with friends and family.

Ingredients:
1 lb boneless, skinless chicken breasts, cut into 1 inch cubes
salt to taste
2 green peppers / capsicums

Marinade:
1 cup greek yogurt
1 tbsp heavy cream (optional)
½ tsp cumin powder
½ cup pistachios (soaked overnight and then ground to a paste)
1-2 green chilli, deseeded and minced
A handful of fresh coriander leaves, finely chopped
2 garlic cloves, minced
½ tsp ginger powder
2 tbsp oil

Marinating:
Combine the marinating ingredients together in a bowl and pour them into a ziplock bag. Add the cubed chicken to the marinade in the bag, rubbing it in, to ensure all the chicken pieces are fully coated. Do not add any salt at this stage. Salt tends to bring out the water from the yogurt, hence it is left until the cooking stage.

Leave the chicken to marinate in the refrigerator overnight or for at least 4-6 hours. If using the wooden barbeque skewers, let these soak in water for at least 20 minutes or longer, before skewing the chicken pieces onto these. If using metal skewers, grease these with a little bit of oil before skewing the chicken pieces.

I like to skew only 4-5 pieces per skewer leaving a little bit of gap between the kebabs.

Cooking:-
The perfect char grilled effect is possible only on the barbeque or in a hot clay oven. However, these can be baked in the oven or shallow fried in a skillet.

Reshmi Kebabs

Literal translation of Reshmi would mean Satin. Creamy satin smooth kebabs that are delicately flavoured and not extra spicy. These are anothe one of my son's favourites.

Ingredients:
1 lb boneless, skinless chicken (thigh meat works best), cut into 1 inch cubes
2 tbsp chick pea flour
1 tbsp ginger powder or 1 ½ inch piece of fresh ginger
3 cloves of garlic, minced
2 fresh green chillies (optional), deseeded and finely chopped
A small bunch of fresh coriander leaves
4 tbsp milk powder
4 tbsp heavy cream
1 egg
2 tbsp lemon juice
3 tbsp butter
3 tbsp coconut powder
½ cup breadcrumbs
1 medium red onion
1 tbsp white pepper
Salt to taste

Method:
Combine and mix all the ingredients in a large bowl really well. Grind the mixture in a food processor a small batch at a time or use a meat grinder.

Grease your hands with some oil and then knead the mixture for a couple of minutes before covering and placing in the refrigerator for at least 4-5 hours or overnight to allow the flavours to marinate well.

When ready to shape the kebabs, make sure you have a bowl of cold water ready as dipping hands in cold water before shaping the kebabs really helps.

The kebabs may be shaped like sausages onto bamboo skewers that have been soaked in water for a couple of hours or onto greased metal skewers. Alternatively, just shape them into small sausages and cook them on a griddle pan, a BBQ or in a preheated oven 375F / 190C / Gas mark 5 until cooked through.

Serve with spicy green mint chutney and a crispy green salad.

Chicken Shwarma

Ingredients:
4 boneless, skinless chicken breasts
2 tbsp cumin coriander powder
1 tbsp red chilli powder
1 tbsp paprika
1 tbsp chaat masala
zest and juice of 1 lemon
4 cloves garlic, minced
1 large onion, thinly sliced
1 red pepper / capsicum, thinly sliced
1 orange or yellow pepper / capsicum, thinly sliced
2 green chillies, finely chopped (optional)
2 tbsp tahini paste
½ cup spicy garlic mayonnaise
1 cup greek yogurt
4 pitas
salt and freshly ground black pepper to taste

Method:
In a Ziploc bag combine all the dry spices, the garlic, the lemon zest and half of the lemon juice. Make a couple of slits on the thickest parts of the chicken breasts and add them to the zip loc bag to marinate. Let it rest in the refrigerator for at least an hour, but preferably overnight for the flavours to incorporate into the chicken.

Cook the chicken in a preheated oven at 375F / 190C / Gas Mark 5, on a lightly greased baking sheet for 20 minutes or until the chicken is fully cooked through. Remove from the oven, let it cool before slicing thinly.

In a small bowl combine the tahini, yogurt, spicy garlic mayonnaise, salt, freshly ground black pepper, the reserved lemon juice and a little drizzle of extra virgin olive oil (completely optional). Mix well and set aside until ready to use.

Heat oil in a large skillet or pan, add the green chillies, onions and peppers and sauté until they soften a little bit. Sprinkle some salt and black pepper to taste. Remove from heat and set aside.

Warm up the Pitas on a hot skillet before assembling the shwarma. To assemble, spread a little of the yogurt sauce on the pita, then add some of the onion and pepper mixture. Spread some of the chicken slices and a dollop of the yogurt sauce on top. Some lightly roasted sesame seeds on the sauce would also work wonders!

Delicious/healthy with salad. Make sure to chill b4 cooking.

Serena's Baked Chicken Strips

This recipe is dedicated to my gorgeous 5 year old niece Serena, for she loves chicken strips, just like her mama! It reminds me of the days when my sister would refuse to eat anything but fried chicken as she used to get withdrawl symptoms after a few days.

Ingredients:
4 boneless, skinless chicken breasts, cut into strips
Spicy garlic mayonnaise
½ tsp freshly ground black pepper
1 tsp paprika
½ tsp red chilli powder (optional and adjust to taste)
2 tsp cumin coriander powder
Salt to taste
1 cup panko flakes / bread crumbs
¼ cup fresh coriander leaves, finely chopped

Method:
I like to use disposable aluminium pie containers for this, as they are shallow and it saves on cleaning up. But you may use any shallow bowl that you may have.

In one bowl, combine the spicy garlic mayonnaise with all the dry spices. In another bowl, mix the breadcrumbs or panko flakes with the fresh coriander and a little salt and freshly ground black pepper.

Taking one strip at a time, coat each strip with the mayonnaise and then dip it in the breadcrumbs, turning over to coat both sides. Place the coated strips onto a greased baking tray or sheet, but it must be of a size that can fit it into your refrigerator. Once all the chicken strips are coated, place the baking sheet into the refrigerator and let it sit for at least 1 hour or preferably for 3-4 hours.

Preheat oven to 375F / 190C / Gas Mark 5. Spray the chicken strips with a little oil and bake in oven for about 10-15 minutes or until they are a lovely golden in colour and fully cooked through.
Serve these with a sweet chilli sauce or make a wrap and serve with some freshly chopped salad.

Honey Spiced Chicken Skewers

Ingredients:
4 boneless, skinless chicken breasts, cut into 1 inch cubes (750 gms)
½ cup honey
½ cup soy sauce
1 tsp freshly ground black pepper
1 tbsp cumin coriander powder
4 tbsp oil
4 cloves of garlic, minced
4 green chillies, minced
2 small onions, cut into 2 inch cubes
1 green pepper / capsicum, cut into cubes
1 red pepper / capsicum, cut into cubes
salt to taste

Method:
In a large bowl, combine all the spices and the honey, soy sauce and green chillies. Whisk well and reserve a little of the sauce to brush onto the kebabs whilst grilling.

Add the chicken. Let marinate in the refrigerator for at least 3 hours, but preferably overnight.

Drain and discard the excess marinade from the chicken and the vegetables. Thread the chicken and the vegetables alternatively onto metal skewers or wooden skewers that have been soaked in water for at least an hour beforehand.

Ideally use the BBQ and grill the kebabs, basting with the sauce a couple of times through the cooking.

Alternatively, bake in a preheated oven 375F / 180C / Gas mark 5 for 12-15 minutes. Brush the kebabs with the reserved marinade and place under the broiler for a few minutes to crisp up the edgs.

Serve with naan bread or with rice and salad.

Chicken Tikka Turnovers
Amazing spicy turnovers are a hit every time I make them

Ingredients:
1 small onion, finely chopped
1 tsp ginger paste
1 green chilli, finely chopped (optional)
2 cups chicken tikka boti (for recipe page 29), roughly chopped
2 tbsp oil
1 tsp cumin seeds
1 packet puff pastry
1 egg, lightly whisked with a tsp of milk
salt and black pepper to taste
(puff pastry is usually salty so I try not to add any more salt to the tikka)

Method:
In a small pan or skillet heat the oil and saute the onions, cumin seeds and the green chilli. Add the ginger paste and cook until the onions have softened and turned a light golden in colour. Add the chicken tikka and remove from heat. Stir in some salt and black pepper to taste, and if you like it extra spicy a little bit of sriracha sauce works wonderfully! Allow to cool.

Preheat oven to 400F / 200C / Gas mark 6.

Roll out the puff pastry if its not in the form of a sheet, to a rectangle shape on a lightly floured surface. Using a knife mark out 4-6 inch squares on the pastry, depending on the size of your sheet or the size that you would like the turnovers to be. I like them small and spicy, so I make mine 4 inch squares.

Spoon a little bit of the chicken mixture almost in the middle of the square, brush some of the egg wash all around the sides and turn it over into a triangle. Press the edges lightly to help them seal. Place them on a lightly greased baking tray with at least a couple of inches gap between them. Brush the top of the turnover with some egg and make a tiny slit at the top of the turnover to allow air to escape in the cooking process.

Serve hot with some mint chutney and spicy ketchup.

Chicken Tikka Turnovers

Chicken Pakoras

Chicken Pakoras
A crowd pleaser and perfect party finger food

2 lbs boneless, skinless chicken breast, cut into thin long strips
½ cup Plain Flour / All purpose Flour

Marinade:
4 tbsp warm milk
1 tsp ginger powder
1 tsp garlic salt
1 tsp red chilli powder
1 tsp harissa paste (optional)
1 tbsp cumin coriander powder
1 tsp black pepper
a few strands of saffron (optional)
salt to taste

Batter:
½ cup chickpea flour / gram flour (besan)
2 tbsp rice flour
½ tsp lightly roasted cumin seeds
½ tsp chicken masala
½ tsp turmeric powder
¼ tsp baking soda
2 tbsp plain yogurt
lukewarm water
salt to taste

Preparation:
Taking a small ramekin size bowl, soak the saffron with the milk and keep this aside.
Pat the chicken dry using some kitchen paper.

Take two zip lock bags. Fill the first one up with the plain flour. The second bag is to be filled up with the ingredients for the marinade including the saffron soaked milk. Zip up the bag carefully and give it a good shake. Massage the ingredients from outside the bag to ensure they are thoroughly mixed.

First drop the chicken pieces into the first bag with the plain flour. Zip up the bag and give it a good shake to ensure all the pieces are evenly coated. Now remove each piece carefully and drop them into the second bag filled with the marinade.

Leave these to marinate in the refrigerator for at least 2 hours upto a maximum of 12 hours or overnight.

To start off the batter, sieve the flours and the dried spices into a large bowl. Whisk together and now add the yogurt and the water. The batter needs to be quite thick, like a pancake batter and should coat the back of a spoon. Let the batter sit aside for 15-20 minutes. Give it another whisk before using.

Preheat the oil in a frying pot to 350-375°F /180-190°C. Check the temperature using a candy thermometer. Whilst the oil is heating, get a baking sheet, cover it completely with aluminium foil for ease of cleaning and place a wire rack in the centre. Keep this aside.

Mindfully Spiced Chicken • Page 39

Take a few kitchen towels and place them on a plate, as this will soak up any excess oil from the pakoras. The oven would need to be preheated to 300F/ 150C / Gas mark 2.

Method:
Dip the marinated chicken cubes one by one into the batter before frying them in the oil. If using a deep fryer, using kitchen tongs hold the piece of chicken on the surface of the oil for a couple of seconds before sliding it into the oil. By letting the batter on one side of the pakora cook in the oil before dropping the piece, the pakora will not drop to the bottom of the deep fryer and make a mess in the oil by getting stuck to the bottom. Just lightly move the pakora using the tongs, in a fan like motion over the surface of the oil. Deep fry 6-8 pakoras at a time, and whilst it is tempting to fry a bigger batch, they will not get crisp if overcrowded in the fryer.

Let the pakoras cook until golden in colour and place them on the plate with kitchen paper to allow the excess oil to drain off onto the paper. Then using the tongs place them on the wire rack above the baking tray.

Once all the pakoras have been fried, put them in the oven for 10 minutes. This will help crisp them up and ensure they are cooked through.

Serve these pakoras hot, with a spicy sauce and a sweet chutney.

Dad's Chicken Chaat

My Dad helped me recreate one of our favourite recipes, which is originally based on the famous Chicken Chaat served at the Volgas Restaurant in Connaught Place, New Delhi. Its a super easy and quick recipe, and it can easily be transformed into a salad by adding fresh salad ingredients.

Ingredients:
2 lb boneless, skinless chicken breasts, cut into thin strips
1 medium sized red onion, finely chopped
2 medium sized tomatoes, deseeded and finely chopped
1 tbsp chaat masala
salt to taste
a handful of fresh mint leaves
a handful of fresh coriander leaves
2 green chillies, finely chopped
2 inch fresh ginger, grated
2 cloves of garlic, minced
freshly ground black pepper
zest and juice of 1 lemon
1 tsp mango powder / amchoor
1 tbsp cumin coriander powder
½ cup fresh pomegranates (optional) as a garnish
2 tbsp oil

Method:
Heat oil in a pan skillet and saute the onions, ginger and garlic until the onions soften. Add the chicken pieces. Sprinkle the lemon zest, a little salt and squeeze half the lemon juice onto the chicken. Reduce the heat to low, cover the pan and allow the chicken to cook for 5 minutes.

It is imperative that the chicken cooks without drying out, and I find that I may need to sprinkle some water onto the chicken sometimes to help build the steam in the pan for the chicken to cook. Check the chicken and if necessary sprinkle some water to help retain the moisture.

As soon as the chicken is cooked, remove from heat and transfer the chicken to a bowl. Sprinkle all the spices, herbs and the green chillies. Squeeze the remaining lemon juice on top. Add the finely chopped tomatoes and serve garnished with the pomegranate seeds.

I like lots of chaat masala on my chicken chaat and extra lemon juice, as well as a few drops of jalapeno tabasco sauce on top!

Chicken 65

Super spicy and ever so addictive. A deep fried spicy chicken recipe very popular as a bar snack in Southern India. If you don't like it so spicy, just reduce the quantitiy of red chilli powder in the recipe to suit your taste, but the dramatic red colour of the chicken does wonders for the party buffet. My twist is adding the white wine to the gravy which works wonders for the flavour. Perfect for a game night with the beers!

Ingredients:
1 lb boneless, skinless chicken breasts cut into 1 inch cubes

Marinade:
1 egg
3 tbsp corn flour
1 tsp white pepper
1 tsp red chilli powder
1 tbsp white vinegar
salt to taste

Gravy:
3 cloves garlic, minced
1 inch piece of ginger, grated
2 tbsp tomato puree / paste
2 tbsp tomato ketchup
1 cup sweet white wine
1 tbsp red chilli powder (optional, adjust to taste)
1 tbsp red chilli flakes (optional, adjust to taste)
a couple of drops of red food colour (optional)
½ tsp turmeric powder
Salt to taste

Method:
Combine all the marinade ingredients in a zip loc bag and add the chicken cubes. Massage the bag gently from outside to help the marinade work its magic and leave it to rest in the refrigerator for at least 1 hour. Deep fry the chicken in hot oil, until golden in colour and cooked through.

Heat oil in a pan and add the chopped ginger and garlic. Saute for a minute on medium high heat, then reduce the heat and stir in the tomato puree/ paste followed by the white wine. Add the remaining spices as well as the ketchup into the gravy followed by the deep fried chicken pieces.

Cover and let this simmer until the gravy thickens. Garnish with chopped green chillies, fresh coriander leaves and very thinly sliced red onion rings. Sprinkle a little bit of chaat masala on top and a little lemon juice and you have a fantastic game night or party dish.

Chicken Shashlik Kebabs

These shallow fried kebabs are popular Indo-Chinese kebabs, and the ingredients reflect the strong Chinese influence on the cuisine. Easy to make and spicylious.

1 lb boneless, skinless chicken breasts, cut into 1 inch cubes
1 green pepper / capsicum, cut into 1 inch cubes
1 large red onion, cut into 1 inch cubes
1 beef tomato, deseeded and cut into 1 inch cubes
2 egg whites, whisked until light and foamy
3 tbsp chilli garlic sauce
3 tbsp oyster sauce
1 tbsp dark soy sauce
1 tsp white vinegar
1 tbsp red chilli powder (optional)
6 cloves of garlic, minced
1 tsp freshly ground black pepper
salt to taste (bearing in mind the soy sauce and oyster sauce are salty in taste)

Method:
Combine all the sauce and spice ingredients in a large bowl and add the chicken to marinade. Let the chicken marinate for 20 minutes before adding the peppers, onions and tomato cubes to the marinate. Let this rest for another 20 minutes.

Thread the kebabs onto skewers, alternating the chicken with the vegetables.

Dip the kebabs in the beaten foamy egg whites, ensuring both sides are fully coated before shallow frying them in hot oil.

These can be baked in the oven, but the flavour from the shallow frying of the kebabs is amazing. Cook until the chicken is fully cooked through.

Serve on a platter with naan bread and a fresh green salad.

Handi Kebab

These kebabs are shallow fried in a pan and then cooked in a creamy yogurt and tomato sauce. Lovely to have with rice at any time of the day.

Ingredients:
For the kebabs:
1 lb chicken mince
1 small onion, finely chopped
1 tbsp ginger garlic paste
2 green chillies, deseeded and finely chopped
1 tbs cumin coriander powder
½ cup breadcrumbs
1 tsp red chilli powder
salt to taste
2 tbsp oil + more for shallow frying

For the gravy:
4 plum tomatoes, finely chopped or 1 can of crushed / chopped tomatoes
1 cup greek yogurt
1 tsp turmeric powder
1 green chilli, slit lengthways (optional)
a handful of fresh coriander leaves, finely chopped
1 tsp chicken masala

Method:
Combine all the kebab ingredients in a large bowl and run it through a meat grinder or a food processor, a small batch at a time. Grease your hands with oil, then dip them in water before kneading the kebab mixture for a minute or two to help combine the ingredients. Let the meat mixture rest in the refrigerator for at least half and hour before making the kebabs.

Wet your hands in cold water before handling the meat, and shape them into a sausage like shape.

Heat some oil in a pan and shallow fry the kebabs until they are cooked through. Remove them from the cooking pan and set aside.

Using the left over oil from the shallow frying in the pan, fry the tomatoes and cook them until they soften. Add the salt, turmeric, chicken masala and the green chilli and continue cooking on medium heat for 2-5 minutes until the tomatoes soften. Stir in the yogurt and continue stirring continuously whilst the yogurt infuses into the tomato gravy. Cook until the oil separates from the yogurt gravy.

Add the kebabs into this gravy, cover, reduce heat and let them simmer for at least 5-10 minutes.

Garnish with fresh coriander leaves and serve hot on a bed of rice with some fresh naan bread.

Tunday Kebabs

These Kebabs are traditionally made with minced mutton, but I am making the healthier option by making them with chicken mince and replacing clarified butter with grapeseed oil. Originating from the traditional Awadhi cuisine in India, they have a distinct flavour of their own.

Ingredients:
2 lbs chicken mince
2 eggs
1 cup bread crumbs
1 large onion, roughly chopped
½ tsp cinnamon powder
2 tsp cumin coriander powder
1 tsp freshly ground black pepper
10 cloves garlic, halved
6 green chillies, halved (adjust to taste)
2 red chillies, halved (optional)
½ cup chana dal (gram/ chick pea lentils) soaked overnight
2 tbsp raw papaya
½ tsp clove powder
½ tsp cardamom powder
oil to shallow fry

Method:
Heat a pot with 3 cups of water and a teaspoon of salt. Crumble the chicken mince into this water and boil the minced chicken until the meat is tender. Drain any excess water and keep aside.

In a food processor, first grind the onion, garlic, chillies to a fine paste. Add the minced chicken and grind the meat to a fine paste. Keep aside in a bowl.

Grind the soaked lentils, the breadcrumbs and all remaining ingredients (except for the eggs) and grind to a paste. Combine with the meat really well. Since this mixture gets a little dry and sticky, I liberally rub some oil over my hands before I handle these kebabs.

Add the eggs and form a dough from the meat. Ideally its best to refrigerate the meat at this point for an hour or so for it to cool down before shaping into small patties or kebabs.

Shallow fry these kebabs till golden brown in colour and serve with a spicy onion salad and mint chutney.

Seekh Kebabs

Kebabs are not complete without seekh kebabs, and every family has their own secret recipe. For a lot of families, the men are in charge of making seekh kebabs on the BBQ for the family and they all have their little twist and a secret ingredient to make their kebabs unique. One of our family friends who makes amazing kebabs, accidentally let slip that his secret was drowsing the kebabs with alcohol ! He used a wee drab of his favourite Bacardi when he made the kebab dough and then liberally brushed it onto the kebabs as he slow cooked them on a charcoal BBQ. I still remember the look of horror on all the 'Auntijees' faces when he revealed his kebabs were liberally laced with alcohol.

My seekh kebabs are simple homemade seekh kebabs, and if you fancy making them boozy go ahead and use some bacardi !

Ingredients:
2 lbs minced chicken
2 medium size onions, minced
6 green chillies, minced
2 inch piece of ginger, grated
4 cloves of garlic, minced
a handful of fresh coriander leaves, finely chopped
a handful of fresh mint leaves, finely chopped
1 tbsp red chilli powder (adjust to taste)
½ tsp freshly ground black pepper
1 tbsp chicken masala
2 tbsp cumin coriander powder
3 tbsp chick pea flour
salt to taste
1 egg, lightly beaten
2 tbsp melted butter

Method:
Dry roast the chick pea flour on a skillet, stirring continuously or it will burn. Let the chick pea flour roast until it turns a golden brown.

Combine all the ingredients in a large bowl and knead it well. If the mixture is too sticky, then you may need to add a little more roasted chick pea flour. Do not add it in without roasting, as it has a very floury texture when not roasted.

Using wet hands, shape the kebabs on presoaked bamboo skewers and ideally cook these on the BBQ. However, an oven works just as well. Place the skewers on a wire rack placed over a baking sheet and cook in a preheated oven at 400F / 200C/ Gas mark 6 for 5 minutes. Brush with a little more melted butter (or alcohol) and return to cook for a further 5 minutes, or until cooked through.

Wings and Drummettes

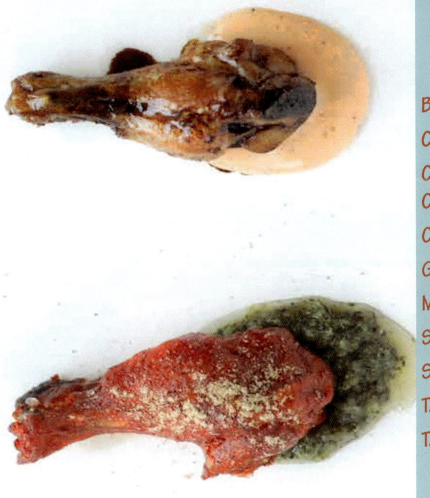

Black Pepper & Cumin Wings

Cajun Mango Wings

Creamy Green Chilli Drummettes

Crunchy Drummettes

Curried Apple Wings

Green Chilli & Paneer Wings

Mango Balsamic Drummettes

Silky Almond Drummettes

Spicy Sweet Garlic Wings

Tandoori Drummettes

Tandoori Roast Chicken Legs

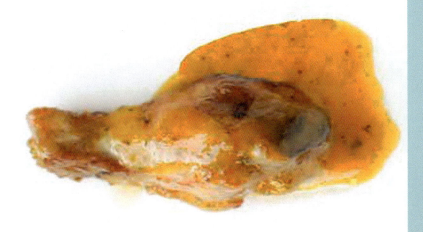

Black Pepper and Cumin Wings

I have modified my mums cumin chicken wings recipe with this peppery and spicy version drizzled with some finger licking smooth sweet mango chutney

Ingredients:
16 chicken wings
½ cup plain flour / all purpose flour
1 tsp red chilli powder (adjust according to taste)
1 tsp cumin powder
2 tsp cumin seeds
2 tsp freshly ground black pepper
1 tsp garam masala
2 tbsp oil
salt to taste

Half a cup mango chutney (for recipe see page 102)

Method:
Wash the chicken wings, drain the water and pat them dry using kitchen paper. Using a sharp knife make a little incision on the thickest part of the wings, so as to assist the spices in marinating through the chicken.

Combine the flour with all the dry spices and marinate the chicken with the flour mixture in a zip lock bag. Massage the chicken wings from outside the bag for a minute or two, before placing it in a refrigerator for at least 2 hours.

The wings can now be deep fried at 360F until golden brown in colour and then baked in the oven for a further 10 minutes at 375F / 190C / Gas mark 5 to ensure they are fully cooked and crisp.

There are two ways to add the chutney to the wings. If you like your wings sticky then you must pour the mango chutney in a large bowl along with the wings, cover and give them a good shake to ensure all the wings are thoroughly covered. Alternatively, if you do not like the stickiness, then warm the chutney for 30 seconds in the microwave before drizzling over the wings very lightly. Serve the remaining chutney in a small bowl as a dip for the wings.

Cajun Mango Wings

I inadvertently married my cajun style spices with a bit of mango pulp, and I have been repeating this mistake ever since for some crispy sweet and spicy wings.

Ingredients:
16 chicken wings
½ cup lemon juice
rind of 1 lemon
1 cup mango pulp
1 tsp red chilli powder
1 tsp paprika
1.5 tsp onion powder
1.5 tsp garlic powder
¼ tsp mustard powder
½ tsp cumin powder
2 tbsp oil
salt and black pepper to taste

Method:
Wash the chicken wings, drain the water and pat them dry using kitchen paper. Using a sharp knife make a little incision on the thickest part of the wings, so as to assist the spices in marinating through the chicken.

Combine all the dry spices, including the salt and black pepper. Divide the dry spices into two equal halves.

Combine the lemon juice, mango pulp and oil with one half of the spice mix, and marinate the chicken in a zip lock bag. Massage the chicken wings from outside the bag for a minute or two, before placing it in a refrigerator for at least 2 hours and upto 24 hours.

Remove the chicken from the zip lock bag and spread out on a wire rack, placed over a baking sheet. Sprinkle the remaining spice mix onto the wings, and the chicken can now be shallow fried, baked in the oven or grilled on a BBQ.

Bake in a hot preheated oven 375F / 190C / Gas mark 5/190C for 25 minutes or shallow fry for about 6-8 minutes on each side, or until the chicken wings are thoroughly cooked.

Serve with a spicy mango chutney and mint chutney.

Creamy Green Chilli Drummettes

Squeeze extra lemon juice until its dripping all over the plate and sprinkle some chaat masala or mango powder on top, roll the drummette in the spicy lemon juice before taking a bite into these juicy, creamy, tangy and spicy drummettes.

Ingredients:
8 chicken drumsticks, skins removed
1 inch piece of ginger
4 cloves of garlic
1 cup of greek yogurt
½ cup of thick heavy Cream (whipping Cream)
½ cup of cream cheese
1 egg
½ tsp garam masala powder
½ tsp fennel powder
A pinch of cardamom powder (optional)
2 green chillies (deseeded - optional)
2 tbsp of chopped fresh coriander leaves
½ tsp coriander powder
salt and black pepper to taste
A tiny pinch of sugar
3 tbsp melted butter

Method:
Wash the chicken drumsticks, drain the water and pat them dry using Kitchen paper. Using a sharp knife make two little incisions on the thickest part of the wings, so as to assist the spices in marinating through the Chicken.
Peel and chop the ginger and garlic before blitzing them in a blender. Add the green chillies, the dry spices, the cream cheese and the egg next and pulse them to a thick paste. Add the remaining ingredients and pulse until they are thoroughly combined.
Pour the marinade into a ziplock bag and add the Chicken drumsticks. Massage them from outside the bag and place them in the refrigerator to marinate for at least 4 hours and for a maximum of 24 hours.

Whilst it is not necessary but it works best if you massage them a few more times through the 24 hours whilst they are marinating, as it really works the creamy marinade into the Chicken.

Preheat the oven to 350F. Place a wire rack over a baking sheet and lightly grease the wire rack. Sprinkly about 1é2 a cup of water onto the bottom of the tray, for added moisture.

Spread the Chicken drumsticks out evenly onto the wire rack and using a sheet of aluminium foil cover the entire baking sheet loosely, crunch up the sides of the foil carefully so as not to let the steam escape. Cook in the oven for 25 minutes.

Remove the foil cover, brush the drumsticks with a little bit of melted butter all around before returning them to the oven to cook for a further 15 minutes or until they are golden and crisp from the outside.

Serve hot with a Red Onion salad and lemon wedges.

Crunchy Drumsticks
Lemony crunchy and spicy baked chicken drumsticks

Ingredients:
2 tbsp grated lemon zest
½ cup fresh lemon juice
3 tbsp packed light brown sugar
1/3 cup buttermilk
12 skin on chicken drumsticks
Salt and black pepper to taste
2 cups panko breadcrumbs
1 tbsp fresh cilantro stems - chopped finely
½ tsp cayenne pepper or red chilli powder
½ tsp coriander powder
½ tsp cumin powder
1 tsp chaat masala
¼ cup mayonnaise
oil cooking spray

Method:
Using a sharp knife make 2 slits on the surface of the drumsticks but don't slice it through, as the slits would help the chicken marinate fully.

Mix together the cumin powder, coriander powder, salt and chilli powder or cayenne pepper in a small bowl and rub this into the slits of the drumsticks.

Mix one tablespoon of the lemon zest with the lemon juice in a small bowl. Add the sugar and 1 cup of water. Dissolve the sugar using a whisk and pour this into the ziplock bag together with the buttermilk.

Drop the drumsticks into the zip lock bag and seal it carefully. Massage the drumsticks from outside the bag very gently so as to mix the marinate and place the bag in the fridge overnight or for at least 5 hours.

Remove the chicken from the fridge about 10 minutes before you are ready to cook.

Preheat the oven to 400F / 200C/ Gas mark 6 and bake the chicken on a lightly greased baking sheet for at least 20 minutes or until the chicken has cooked through. You may need to turn over the chicken after the first 10 minutes.

Serve with a spicy tomato ketchup and mint chutney.

Curried Apple Chicken Wings

Ingredients:
16 chicken wings
1 cup unsweetened applesauce (homemade or store bought)
½ tsp freshly ground black pepper
½ tsp cumin powder
½ tsp red chilli powder
1 tsp curry powder
2 tbsp lemon juice
1 tbsp fresh coriander, finely chopped
2 tbsp oil
salt to taste

Method:
Wash the chicken wings, drain the water and pat them dry using kitchen paper. Using a sharp knife make a little incision on the thickest part of the wings, so as to assist the spices in marinating through the chicken.

Combine all the dry spices, including the salt and blend these into the applesauce using a fork. Add the lemon juice and oil.

Add all ingredients into a zip lock bag and add the chicken wings. Massage the chicken wings from outside the bag for a minute or two, before placing it in a refrigerator for at least 2 hours and upto 24 hours.

Remove the chicken from the zip lock bag and shallow fry, bake or grill these on a BBQ.

Bake in a hot preheated oven 375F / 190C / Gas Mark 5 for 25 minutes or shallow fry for about 6-8 minutes on each side, or until the chicken wings are thoroughly cooked.

Serve sprinkled with some chaat masala on top.

Green Chilli and Paneer Wings
Twice marinated Tangy Spicy Cheesy Wings

16 chicken wings

First marinade:
3 cloves of garlic, minced
1 inch piece of Ginger, grated
2 fresh green chillies, minced
½ tsp lemon juice
salt to taste

Second marinade:
½ cup crumbled or grated Paneer (Indian cheese or use ricotta cheese)
1 egg white
4 tbsp thick heavy cream
salt and black pepper to taste
1 tsp chicken masala
½ tsp fennel powder

2-3 tbsp melted butter

Method:
Wash the chicken wings, drain the water and pat them dry using kitchen paper. Using a sharp knife make a little incision on the thickest part of the wings, so as to assist the spices in marinating through the chicken.

Blitz all the ingredients for the first marinade in a blender or food processor and pour into a zip lock bag. If you prefer, you may choose to remove the seeds from the green chillies prior to adding them to the marinade. Add the chicken wings and massage them slightly before placing the bag into the refrigerator for 1 hour.

In the meantime, combine the ingredients for the second marinate in a blender and add them to the previously marinated chicken wings in the same zip lock bag. Massage the wings from outside the bag gently and return to the refrigerator for a further 4 hours minimum or upto a maximum of 24 hours.

Preheat the oven to 400F / 200C / Gas mark 6. Lightly grease a wire rack and place it above a baking sheet or tray, prior to spreading the wings on the rack. Discard the excess marinade and do not overload the wings with any extra marinate. This will help the wings crisp up nicely in the oven.

Let the wings roast in the oven for 15 minutes, before removing them and brushing them with some melted butter on both sides. Return to the oven for a further 10 minutes or until they crisp up and are cooked through.

Serve with a crisp green salad drizzled with a spicy vinaigrette.

Mango Balsamic Drummettes

12 chicken drumsticks

Marinade:
½ cup balsamic vinegar
1 cup mango pulp
4 cloves of garlic, minced
1 tsp ginger powder
½ tsp red chilli powder
1 tsp coriander powder
2 tbsp mushroom or medium dark soy sauce
salt and black pepper to taste
(adjust to allow for the salt in the soy sauce)

1 tbsp oil
2 shallots, finely chopped

½ cup fresh coriander leaves, chopped
2 tbsp lightly toasted sesame seeds

Method:
Wash the chicken drumsticks, drain the water and pat them dry using kitchen paper. Using a sharp knife make two little incisions on the thickest part of the drumsticks, so as to assist the spices in marinating through the chicken.

Taking a large zip lock bag, mix all the ingredients thoroughly by shaking and massaging, before adding the chicken drumsticks. Massage the drumsticks from outside the bag.

Let this marinate for at least 2 hours in the refrigerator up to a maximum of 24 hours. The marinade will look a bit watery, but do not discard this when you remove the drumsticks for cooking.

Preheat the oven to 375F / 190C / Gas Mark 5. Cover a baking tray with aluminium foil for ease of cleaning. Place a wire rack over the baking tray and lightly grease the wire rack. Sprinkle about a ¼ cup of water onto the bottom of the tray, for added moisture.

Spread the chicken drumsticks out evenly onto the wire rack and using a sheet of aluminium foil cover the entire baking sheet loosely, crunch up the sides of the foil carefully so as not to let the steam escape. Cook in the oven for 25 minutes.

In the meantime, heat the oil in a small pan on medium high heat and cook the shallots until soft and translucent. Add the marinade from the ziplock bag into the pan for heating. It is imperative that the marinade is brought to a boil as in order to kill bacteria. Once it reaches a boil, reduce the heat to a low simmer and let this cook uncovered, on low heat until the sauce thickens. It should take about 10-15 minutes.

Remove the chicken drumsticks from the oven, and discard the foil covering the drumsticks and return the drumsticks to continue cooking in the oven for a further 10 minutes or until cooked through. Brush the sauce onto the drumsticks whilst they are still hot, making sure they are brushed evenly on both sides. Sprinkle the toasted sesame seeds on top as a garnish.

I like to add some fresh spring onions / green onions as a garnish along with the sesame seeds. Serve with the sweet spicy tomato sauce.

Silky Almond Drummettes

8 chicken drumsticks, skins removed

First marinade:
3 tbsp freshly squeezed lemon juice
3 cloves of garlic, minced
1 tsp ginger powder
1 tsp coriander powder
½ tsp red chilli powder
salt and black pepper to taste

Second marinade:
3 tbsp of heavy thick cream
4 tbsp of greek yogurt
4 tbsp of coarse almond powder
3 tsp of dried fenugreek leaves (*Kasoori Methi*) (optional)
2 tsp of dried coriander leaves
salt to taste

Method:
3 tbsp melted butter mixed in with ½ tsp of fresh chopped or dried coriander leaves

Wash the chicken drumsticks, drain the water and pat them dry using kitchen paper. Using a sharp knife make two little incisions on the thickest part of the wings, so as to assist the spices in marinating through the chicken. Taking a large zip lock bag, mix all the ingredients for the first marinade in the bag and add the chicken drumsticks. Massage the drumsticks from outside the bag so as to assist the spices. Leave these to marinate for an hour in the refrigerator.

Combine the 6 ingredients for the second marinade in a small bowl and add these into the zip lock bag. Massage the bag from the outside to assist the marinade work its magic into the drumsticks.

Preheat the oven to 350F /180C/ Gas mark 4. Place a wire rack over a baking sheet and lightly grease the wire rack. Sprinkly about ½ a cup of water onto the bottom of the tray, for added moisture.

Spread the chicken drumsticks out evenly onto the wire rack and using a sheet of aluminium foil cover the entire baking sheet loosely, crunch up the sides of the foil carefully so as not to let the steam escape. Cook in the oven for 25 minutes.

Remove the foil cover, brush the drumsticks with a little bit of melted butter all around before returning them to the oven to cook for a further 10-15 minutes or until they are golden and crisp from the outside.

Sprinkle some chaat masala on top and serve with a slice of lemon.

Spicy Sweet Garlic Wings

Ingredients:
16 chicken wings
3 tbsp oil
½ cup of finely chopped shallots
8 cloves of crushed garlic
1tsp ginger powder
3 tsp sugar
1 tsp red chilli powder
3 tsp mushroom soy sauce
salt to taste

Method:
Heat oil in a large pan, add the chopped onions and cook these on medium heat, stirring from time to time. The onions should be cooked until they are a light caramel colour.

Add the garlic and continue cooking until the crushed garlic blends in with the onions and takes on a bit of colour. Add the dry spices into this mixture, saving the sugar and soy sauce for later.

Stir the spices well into mixture and reduce the heat. Add the chicken wings and stir them so as to let the onion mixture coat the wings thoroughly. Add a cup of tap water and cover the pan. Let the wings cook in the covered pan on low heat until the wings are cooked.

Depending on the size of the wings, the cooking process should take 10-20 minutes. Check for doneness, but don't let the steam escape too much. Add the sugar and Soy sauce at this point and let the wings cook uncovered on medium high heat for last couple of minutes. If there is excess water, let them cook a little longer to allow the water to evaporate.

I like to garnish these wings with a sprinkling of roasted sesame seeds and finely chopped green onions (spring onions) and a bowl of sweet spicy garlic sauce.

Tandoori Drumsticks

This was one of the first things I learnt to cook, and this recipe is a modified version of the original recipe that I learnt from my cousin who is the 'King of Tandoori Drumsticks' till today.
Instead of basting with butter, we used to liberally baste the drum sticks with a bit of Bacardi specially when cooking on the BBQ and this secret was never shared.

Ingredients:
12 chicken drumsticks
1 cup yogurt
3 tbsp lemon juice
1 tsp ginger powder
2 tbsp tandoori masala
1 tsp coriander powder
½ tsp mango powder (Amchoor)
salt and black pepper to taste
1 tsp oil

3 tbsp melted butter for basting

Method:
Wash the chicken drumsticks, drain the water and pat them dry using kitchen paper. Using a sharp knife make two little incisions on the thickest part of the wings, so as to assist the spices in marinating through the chicken.

Taking a large zip lock bag, mix all the ingredients in the bag (save the butter) and add the chicken drumsticks. Massage the drumsticks from outside the bag. Let this marinate for an hour in the refrigerator. Preheat the oven to 375F / 190C / Gas Mark 5. Place a wire rack over a baking tray and lightly grease the wire rack.

Sprinkly about ½ a cup of water onto the bottom of the tray, for added moisture. Spread the chicken drumsticks out evenly onto the wire rack and using a sheet of aluminium foil cover the entire baking sheet loosely, crunch up the sides of the foil carefully so as not to let the steam escape. Cook in the oven for 25 minutes.

Remove the foil cover, brush the drumsticks with a little bit of melted butter all around before returning them to the oven to cook for a further 10-15 minutes or until they are cooked through.

Serve with a red onion salad, some thinly sliced cucumbers, lemon wedges and sprinkle a pinch of mango powder on top of each drumstick. Mint chutney works beautifully with these drumsticks too.

Variation:
Since these drumsticks were traditionally cooked in the clay oven, these cook fantastically on a BBQ and are a hit at parties. Take a 3inch wide piece of aluminium foil, and wrap it around the thinner end of the drumstick when serving at parties. On average, allow 2-3 pieces per person as an appetiser.

Tandoori Roast Chicken Legs

These twice marinated chicken legs were my grandad's favourites and they form the basis of Papaji's Butter Chicken on page 84. I like to marinate a load of these and keep them handy in the freezer as everyone in our family love these!

4 Chicken legs (thighs attached), skin removed

First marinade:
2 tbsp lemon juice
1 tbsp ginger paste
1 tsp red chilli powder
salt to taste

Second marinade:
1 tbsp garlic paste
1 tsp chicken masala
1 tsp chaat masala
1 tsp dried fenugreek leaves
a couple of drops of red icing colour

Method:
Firstly, make two slits on the thickest part of the chicken thigs and spread the chicken out on kitchen paper. Pat the chicken dry to remove any excess moisture.

Combine the ingredients for the first marinate in a zip loc bag and add the chicken to the bag. Massage the chicken pieces from outside the bag and leave to rest in a refrigerator for at least an hour.

Combine the ingredients for the second marinate and add to the chicken in the zip loc. Massage the chicken pieces for a couple of minutes from outside the bag to ensure the marinate covers the chicken pieces well. Leave to rest in the refrigerator for least 2-3 hours or even overnight.

Preheat the oven to 375F/ 180C / Gas mark 5. Place a wire rack over a baking sheet that has been lined with aluminium foil and place the chicken pieces on the wire rack.

Bake in oven for 5 minutes. Baste the chicken with melted butter and return to the oven. Continue basting with melted butter every 5 minutes until chicken is fully cooked through.

Serve on a bed of salad, and liberally sprinkled with chaat masala and lemon wedges on the side.

Traditional Chicken

Chicken Chasni

Chicken Koftas in creamy rich sauce

Chicken Korma - Delhi Style

Chettinadu Chicken

Pumpkin Chicken

Chicken Chaap

Chicken Dopiaza

Spinach Chicken

Chicken Jalfrezi

Almond Chicken Korma

Degi Chicken Korma

Chicken Tikka Masala - British Style

Lahori Chicken Chickpeas

Mums Chicken Curry

Methi Chicken

Kolhapuri Chicken

Chicken Changezi

Tandoori Jalfrezi

Malabar Chicken Korma

Chicken Vindaloo

Chicken Korma - British Style

Papajis Butter Chicken

Jakey's Butter Chicken

Raj's Yogurt Chicken

Quick Chicken Pulao

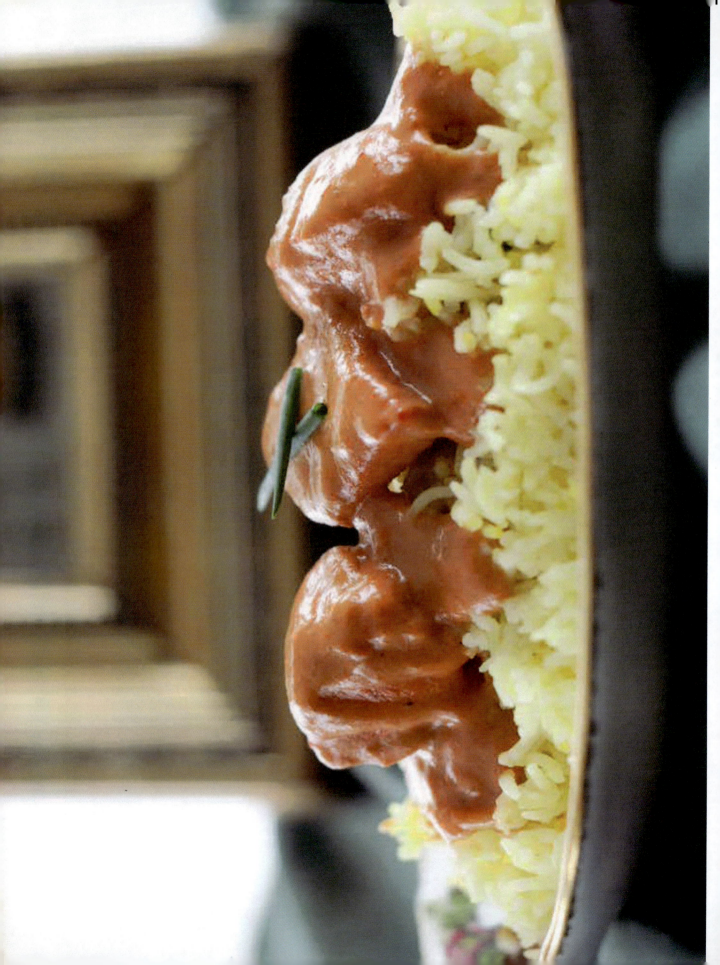

Chicken Chasni

I was a little sceptical when I heard about the Scottish tribute to the Indian cuisine, but it was love at the first morsel. Every trip to Glasgow and Edinburgh for me is incomplete without Chicken Chasni.
The word 'chasni' literally means sugar syrup. But there is no sugar syrup in this recipe!
However the mango pulp makes it a tad sweet, and once you get the balance of the sweet, tangy, spicy, creamy and salty you have an amazing chicken dish.

Ingredients:
4 boneless, skinless chicken breasts (700gms), cut into 1 inch cubes
4 tbsp oil
2 medium onions, minced
2 tsp turmeric powder
1 tsp red chilli powder (adjust to taste)
1 cup mango pulp
1 green chilli, minced
1 inch piece of ginger, minced
1 tsp white pepper
1 tbsp tomato ketchup
2 cups chicken stock
2 tbsp tomato puree/ paste
a few leaves of fresh mint, finely chopped (optional)
½ cup heavy cream
1 tsp chaat masala
salt to taste

Method:
Heat the oil in a medium size pot over medium heat. Add the onions and the minced ginger, until they are golden brown in colour. A small pinch of salt helps expedite this process.

Stir in the spices and the tomato puree, and slowly drizzle some chicken stock in as you stir fry. Reduce the heat and add the chicken cubes. Cover and let it simmer until the chicken is fully cooked.

Combine the mango pulp, ketchup, mint and the cream. Add the creamy mixture to the chicken a little at a time stirring continuously. If the gravy is a little thin, then make a paste using a tbsp of cornflour and cold water and add to the gravy to thicken it.

Serve hot, garnished with a little more cream over a bed of saffron rice to bring a bit of Scottish Indian cuisine into your home.

Chicken Koftas in a creamy rich sauce

These are one of my favourites and I have been known to serve these with spaghetti as my version of spaghetti meatballs, but they are just as good with rice and fresh naan bread.

For the koftas:
1 lb minced chicken
1 small onion, finely chopped
2 green chillies, deseeded and minced (adjust to taste)
4 tbsp fresh coriander, finely chopped
½ tsp red chilli powder (optional)
1 tsp chicken masala
1 tbsp chick pea flour / besan
1 egg
salt and freshly ground black pepper to taste
3 tbsp greek yogurt

For the gravy:
1 large onion, finely chopped
1 cup thick yogurt
2 cloves of garlic, minced
1 tsp ginger paste or ½ inch piece of ginger, grated
1 tbsp cumin coriander powder
1 tbsp chicken masala
½ tsp turmeric powder
1 tsp red chilli powder (optional)
¼ cup oil
2 cups chicken stock
1 green chilli, finely chopped
salt to taste
2 tbsp tomato puree/ paste

Method:
Dry roast the chick pea flour on a skillet on medium heat, stirring continuously to prevent burning until it is golden brown in colour. Set it aside and let it cool. I would suggest roasting a little extra, in case you need some more later.

Combine the ingredients for the koftas and knead it like dough, this ensures it is mixed well. I like to knead it for at least 5 minutes and then refrigerate it in a sealed container for at least one hour. By cooling down the meat mixture, the meatballs can be shaped much easily. If the mixture is too sticky and is not holding together well, then add another tbsp of roasted chick pea flour.

For the gravy, heat oil in a large pot and saute the onions, ginger, the green chilli and garlic. Cook until the onions soften and turn a golden brown in colour. Stir in the spices, the tomato puree and 1 cup of chicken stock. Using a hand blender, blitz the gravy to make it smooth. Continue cooking and add a ¼ cup of yogurt at a time whilst stirring to prevent the yogurt from curdling up. Cook on medium heat until the oil comes up on to the surface.

Drop the meatballs gently into the gravy and no matter what happens, do no use a spoon to stir the gravy. Hold the pot using oven gloves and gently turn the pot around to turn the meatballs. Cook on medium high heat till the first boil. Then cover the pot, reduce the heat to low and let it simmer on low heat for 10 minutes. Sprinkle some fresh coriander leaves on top and stir in some cream for extra love before serving.

Chicken Korma - Delhi style

For all the years that I lived in England, I never liked Korma. It was always too creamy and very mild in flavour. However, when I went to Delhi recently I was pleasantly surprised to find Korma was very different. I discovered that Korma was basically a Mughlai technique where they cooked meat in a blend of spices combined with yogurt, but the trick was to keep the yogurt below curdling temperature. By incorporating the yogurt slowly and carefully into the meat, it combined beautifully with the meat juices. Hence it was cooked on low heat with charcoal on the lid to provide heat evenly.

Whilst I love the flavour, I don't have the time or patience to cook that slow. So this is my uncomplicated cooking tribute to Delhi.

Ingredients:

2 lbs boneless, skinless chicken, cut into 1 inch cubes
1 medium size onion, finely chopped
2 tsp freshly ground black pepper
½ tsp clove powder
½ tsp cardamom powder
1 bay leaf
3 cloves garlic, minced
1 inch piece ginger, grated
1 tsp red chilli powder (optional)
2 green chillies, deseeded and finely chopped
½ cup greek yogurt
1 tbsp cumin coriander powder
½ tsp mace powder
salt to taste
1 tsp turmeric powder
1 tsp chicken masala
1 cup chicken stock
4 tbsp oil

Method:

Heat oil in a pot, add the bay leaf followed by the onions. Sprinkle a pinch of salt to this, as it helps speed up the cooking of the onions. Saute the onions until they are golden in colour and add the ginger, garlic and the green chillies. Reduce the heat and add the chicken pieces.

Continue cooking until the chicken starts to change colour and add all the spices as well as the salt. Stir in a cup of chicken stock and mix well.

Cover and let the chicken simmer for 20 minutes until cooked through. Whisk the yogurt with a fork and add 2 tbsp of milk to the yogurt before adding it to the chicken. Add a little at a time, stirring to help the yogurt blend in with the chicken.

Cook for a further 5 minutes on low heat and if you are having company or are cooking for a special occasion, add ¼ cup of heavy cream and cover until ready to serve.

Garnish with freshly chopped coriander, some fried onions and finely chopped green chillies.

Chettinadu Chicken

A traditional South Indian dish – spicy with a fresh coconut flavour. Don't be intimidated by the long list of ingredients, its worth the effort to make this fantastic dish.

Ingredients:
2 lbs boneless, skinless chicken breasts, cut into 1 inch cubes
2 medium sized onions, finely chopped
2 medium sized tomatoes (or ½ a can of chopped plum tomatoes), finely chopped
2 inch piece of fresh ginger, grated
4 fresh green chillies (adjust to taste), finely chopped
2 green cardamoms, opened and separate the seeds from the shells
Juice and rind of 1 lemon
1 cup unsweetened dessicated coconut (freshly grated coconut would be best if available)
A small bunch of fresh coriander leaves, finely chopped
6 cloves of garlic, minced
2 tbsp poppy seeds
1 tsp turmeric powder
½ tsp garam masala powder
1 tsp coriander powder
1 tsp fennel seeds
¼ tsp cinnamon powder
¼ tsp freshly ground black pepper
1 tsp red chilli powder (adjust to taste)
salt to taste
2 tbsp oil
1 can coconut milk
curry leaves for garnishing (if available)

Preparation:

Dry roast the poppy seeds on a skillet on low heat. Crush in a mortar and pestle or using a rolling pin. Soak in a couple of tablespoons of water and set aside for about 20 minutes.

Dry roast the fennel seeds on a skillet on low heat, stirring all the time to avoid burning. Crush in a mortar and pestle or using a rolling pin and set aside.

In a small bowl, combine the seeds from the cardamom pods, the crushed fennel seeds, cinnamon powder, turmeric powder, coriander powder, black pepper, red chilli powder, the lemon zest, dessicated coconut and the poppy seed mixture. Combine well, adding water as required until a smooth thick paste is ready. Set aside.

Method:

Heat oil in a large pan and sauté the onions until soft and golden in colour. Add the ginger and continue cooking for a further 4-5 minutes before adding the crushed garlic. Lower the heat or the garlic will burn and turn bitter. Add the spice paste and continue cooking for a further 3-4 minutes before adding the chicken.

Stir the chicken well ensuring all the pieces are evenly covered with the spice paste, before stirring in the chopped tomatoes. Add the salt and also stir in the coconut milk.

Cover and cook for about 25 minutes on low to medium heat until the chicken is cooked through. When the chicken is fully cooked, stir in the fresh coriander leaves and the lemon juice. Garnish with fried curry leaves before serving with your choice of rice or naan bread.

Pumpkin Chicken

Left over chicken and a load of Pumpkin, led to the creation of this recipe.

Ingredients:
2 lbs. boneless, skinless chicken, cut into 1 inch cubes
2 cups grated pumpkin
1 medium sized onion, finely chopped
1 inch piece of ginger, grated
2 cloves of garlic, minced
2-3 green chillies, finely chopped
½ tsp red chilli powder
1 tbsp cumin coriander powder
1 tsp cumin seeds
1 tbsp chicken masala
½ cup crushed tomatoes or ½ can of diced tomatoes
1 tbsp tomato puree/ paste
4 tbsp oil
1 tsp turmeric powder

Method:
Put the chicken to boil in a pot, with a bay leaf and not too much water. Heat oil in a pan, add the cumin seeds. 30 seconds later add the onions, the ginger and the green chillies. Sprinkle a pinch of salt onto the onions to help cook them faster, and saute these until the onions are golden brown in colour. Add the garlic and continue to cook.

Add the spices to this mixture, followed by the tomato puree/paste and the crushed tomatoes. Reduce the heat as you stir this well. Add the grated pumpkin, ½ a cup at a time and stir this in well. Take a little bit of the stock from the boiled chicken and stir this into the pumpkin. Cover and let this simmer for 10 minutes.

Stir and check that the pumpkin is not sticking at the bottom of the pan. If it looks too dry, add some more chicken stock. Once the pumpkin has softened and cooked well, it will turn into a bit of a mash. Add the chicken as well as the chicken stock into the pumpkin and cook this until the chicken and the pumpkin have blended well.

For the extra decadence, stir in 1/3 cup of heavy cream and a tbsp of butter. Garnish with finely chopped fresh coriander leaves and enjoy with some freshly baked naan bread.

Chicken Chaap

A traditional rich looking and sinfully delicious gravy made with bone-in chicken pieces. Boneless chicken may be used for this dish, however I would add in a couple of drummettes for the added flavour. If you make this for dinner, save some to eat with Paranthas (fried Indian flat bread) the following morning for breakfast.

Ingredients:
2 lbs bonelss, skinless chicken breasts, cut into 1 inch cubes
4 medium sized onions, finely chopped
2 inch piece of ginger, grated
½ tsp ginger powder
6 cloves garlic, minced
2 tbsp tomato puree or tomato paste
1 cup natural yogurt
1 tbsp rose water
1 tbsp turmeric powder
1 tbsp Kashmiri red chili powder
1 tsp freshly ground black pepper
1 tsp garam masla
1 tsp coriander powder
½ tsp cumin seeds
1 tsp sugar
2 tbsp clarified butter
2 tbsp oil
Salt to taste
3 bay leaves
3 green cardamoms
4 green chillies, finely chopped
2 cloves
1 star aniseed

Method:
In a zip loc bag, marinate the chicken with the ginger powder, yogurt, crushed garlic and salt for 4 hours minimum, but preferably overnight.

Heat oil in a pot, add the bay leaves and the cumin seeds followed by the onions. Sauté till soft and golden brown before adding the ginger and the green chillies. Cook these well stirring continuously. Using a hand blender or a food processor, blend these into a fine smooth paste.

In the same pot, heat the clarified butter and add the onion paste to the pot. Stir in all the dry spices, including the cardamoms, cloves and the sugar. Cook for a couple of minutes before adding the tomato puree or paste. If the mixture looks too dry, add ½ a cup of water and let this cook on medium heat.

Add the marinated chicken, folding into the spice paste well. Reduce the heat to low, cover the pot and let this slowly cook for about 20 minutes and the chicken is fully cooked.

Once the chicken feels tender to touch, stir in the rose water and cover the pot again. Switch off the heat but let the chicken sit in the pot for at least 15 minutes before serving. Sprinkle some fresh coriander leaves before serving, and a couple of green chillies slit lengthways.

Chicken Dopiaza

A traditional heavy onion gravy sauce but I have modernised it without compromising on the taste, to suit fussy eaters who don't like too many onions and spice bits in their food. Since I have a couple of them in my family, I have noticed that they eat this gravy and forget to pick out the few onions that they can see.

Ingredients:
2 lbs boneless, skinless chicken breasts, cut into 1 inch cubes
8 – 10 shallots, peeled
8 – 10 baby potatoes
3 medium size onions, thinly sliced
2 inch piece of fresh ginger, grated
A small bunch of fresh coriander leaves, finely chopped
1 bay leaf
4 cloves of garlic, minced
2-4 green chillies (adjust to taste), finely chopped
2 inch piece of cinnamon stick
4 cloves, crushed
1 tsp freshly ground black pepper
½ cup natural yogurt
6 green cardamoms, smash them slightly to release the flavour, but don't separate the seeds
1 black cardamom, smashed to help release the flavour, but don't remove the seeds
2 tsp turmeric powder
1 tsp garam masala
1 tsp red chilli powder (adjust to taste)
2 tsp chicken masala
4 tbsp oil
2 tsp cumin seeds
2 tsp coriander seeds
1 can chopped tomatoes or 4 plum tomatoes
2 cups chicken stock

Method:
In a zip loc bag, marinate the chicken using the yogurt, a pinch of salt, chilli powder and 1 tsp of the turmeric powder and leave in the refrigerator for at least 3 hours, or preferably overnight.

In a large pan, heat 2 tbsp of oil and to this add the cumin seeds followed 10 seconds later by the coriander seeds and the bay leaf. Add the cardamom pods, cinnamon, cloves and the thinly sliced onions. Cook the onions until soft and golden in colour. Add the ginger, garlic and green chillies and continue cooking for a few minutes. Add the tomatoes and mix well. If the mixture is sticking to the bottom of the pan, sprinkle a couple of tbsp. of water and continue stirring.

Remove the pot from the heat and let this mixture cool for a few minutes before blending into a smooth paste for the gravy. Keep aside.

Heat the pot again and add 2 tbsp of oil and add the shallots. Stir fry until the outer skin of the shallots turn slightly crispy and golden brown in colour. Add the marinated chicken to the pot and cook for 3-4 minutes before adding the potatoes and the gravy paste. Mix well and stir in the chicken stock and the remaining dried spices. Reduce the heat, cover the pot and let this simmer on low heat for at least 20-25 minutes or until the chicken and the potatoes are cooked through.

Finally add some salt and sprinkle the fresh coriander leaves. Stir well, cover the pot and let the chicken rest for a couple of hours before heating again to serve hot. Garnish with fried onions, slit green chillies and fresh coriander leaves.

Spinach Chicken

aka Saag Chicken. If I have left over chicken in the fridge, and some frozen spinach, this is another one of my favourite things to make.

Ingredients:
2 lbs boneless, skinless chicken breasts, cut into 1 inch cubes
2 medium size onions, finely chopped
4 green chillies, finely chopped
1 kg fresh spinach, washed, thick stems removed and finely chopped
(alternatively, use frozen chopped spinach, it works just as well and so does the canned spinach)
2 inch piece of ginger, grated
6 cloves garlic, minced
2 tbsp cumin coriander powder
2 tsp turmeric powder
1 cup crushed tomatoes, or diced tomatoes
2 tbsp tomato puree/ paste
1 tbsp chicken masala
1 tbsp garam masala
1 tsp freshly ground black pepper
salt to taste
Butter and clarified butter (optional)
4 tbsp oil
1 cup chicken stock
1 tbsp cumin seeds

Method:
Heat a pot on medium heat, add the oil and add the cumin seeds. As they start to sizzle, add the onions, ginger and green chillies. Saute the onions until they soften and turn a golden brown in colour. Add the garlic and continue to saute for a further minute, before adding the tomatoes, the tomato paste and the dried spices (except for the garam masala). Stir in the chicken, along with half a cup of the chicken stoccck. Reduce the heat, cover the pot and let this simmer for a few minutes.

In the meantime, take another pot and add the spinach to this pot along with the remaining chicken stock. I add the spinach a bunch at a time, as it gives it time to wilt before I add the next batch. Once all the spinach has softened and wilted, reduce the heat and cover the pot. Allow the spinach to simmer for about 10 minutes. If you don't like the leafy texture of spinach, use a hand blender and blitz the spinach to a smooth paste. Return the spinach paste to the pot, along with a couple of tablespoons of butter or clarified butter. Reduce the spinach on medium high heat, stirring from time to time so that all the excess water evaporates. This can take upto 20-25 minutes but its worth the hard work.

Once the spinach feels drier and plumpier, combine it with the chicken and sprinkle the garam masala on top. Stir well, cover the pot, and let it simmer for a further 20-25 minutes, but check every 5 minutes to make sure it is not sticking at the bottom.

Variation:
To give it some extra love like my mum would, take half a cup of clarified butter in a wok. Heat the wok on medium high until its quite hot, and add some of the spinach chicken to this about a quarter of the quantity at a time, and stir fry this on high heat. Serve with a dollop of whipped butter on top for that extra zing. Unfortunately, our hearts can't take that much love very often.

Serve with a fresh crispy naan bread.

Chicken Jalfrezi
Literal meaning of Jalfrezi means a quick stir fry. Traditionally this dish is made crispy and spicy.

Ingredients:
2 lbs boneless, skinless chicken cut into 1 inch cubes
3 green peppers, cut into 1 inch cubes
1 large onion, cut into 1 inch cubes
1 can chopped tomatoes or 4 plum tomatoes
4-6 green chillies (adjust to taste), finely chopped
2 cups chicken stock
1 tbsp cumin seeds
10 cloves of garlic, minced
2 tbsp tomato puree or paste
2 tsp turmeric powder
½ cup yogurt
4 tbsp oil
1 tsp red chilli powder (optional)
1 tsp garam masala
A small bunch of fresh coriander leaves
salt to taste

Method:
In a large pot, heat 2 tbsp of oil oil and add the cumin seeds. Fry these for 10-15 seconds and add the garlic and green chillies. Stir occasionally and cook these for a minute or so.

Add the tomatoes and continue cooking, stirring regularly. Stir in the turmeric powder, the red chilli powder (if using) and some salt. As the sauce thickens, add the chicken pieces and mix well, ensuring the pieces are all coated with the sauce. Stir in the yogurt and the chicken stock, reduce the heat, cover the pot and let the chicken simmer for 20-25 minutes until cooked through.

In another pan or wok, heat 2 tbsp of oil, add the onions and stir fry these for a couple of minutes before adding in the peppers and stirring in some salt and the garam masala. Stir continuously until the onions and ppers slightly soften and add the tomato puree or past. You may need to sprinkle a couple of spoons of water to this, depending on the thickness of the paste. Reduce the heat and combine with the chicken gravy as soon as the chicken has cooked through.

Sprinkle a generous amount of chopped fresh coriander onto the Jalfrezi. Serve immediately, garnished with fresh coriander, green chillies and tomato wedges.

Almond Chicken Korma

Another Korma that I fell in love with when I went to Delhi. Tender succulent chicken in this creamy almond sauce with a spicy tingle is yet another unforgettable dish, that traditionally came into Indian cuisine thanks to the Mughals. Ideally, if you can, make this using a whole chicken cut into pieces or ask your butcher to do it for you. It makes a world of difference to the flavour. I tend to mix half boned pieces with half boneless breasts to keep children happy.

Ingredients:
2 lbs boneless, skinless chicken breasts, cut into 1 inch cubes
2 large onions, sliced very thinly
7 tbsp oil
1 tbsp cardamom powder
½ tsp clove powder
½ tsp cinnamon powder
¼ tsp mace powder
½ tsp nutmeg
2 inch piece of ginger, grated
6 cloves garlic, minced
1 cup greek yogurt, lightly whisked
4 green chillies, minced (adjust to taste)
1 tsp red chilli powder (adjust to taste)
35-40 almonds
2 tbsp rose water
salt to taste
¼ cup heavy cream (optional)
a handful of fresh coriander leaves, finely chopped
½ cup white wine (optional)

Method:
Heat 3 tbsp oil in a heavy base pan and saute the onions on medium heat. Sprinkle a little salt on the onions to expedite the process and cook until the onions soften and turn golden brown in colour. Blend these onions to a smooth paste, when they cool down using a tbsp of yogurt and set aside.

Mix all the spices together in a little bowl and using a little water blend it to a paste, making sure there are no lumps. Keep aside.

In a small bowl, soak the almonds in boiling water for a few minutes. Drain the water and remove the skins off the almonds. It should just peel off quite easily. Chop half the almonds into thin slivers and grind the other half using a little oil to make a thick paste. Set aside.

Heat 4 tbsp oil in a heavy base pan (or a Dutch oven) and saute the green chillies, garlic, ginger for 1-2 minutes before adding the chicken. I like to add a little white wine at this point, but you may add water if you prefer. Stir in the reserved spice paste into the chicken followed by the yogurt. Reduce the heat, cover the pot and let the chicken simmer for 20 minutes or so on low heat.

Stir in the onion paste, the almond paste, rose water and half the almond slivers. Cover the pot again and let it simmer for a further 5 minutes. Serve garnished with fresh coriander leaves and the reserved almond slivers on top. A little drizzle of cream would add extra love to the dish, but thats optional.

Degi Chicken Korma

A traditional red korma influenced by the Mughlai cuisine and popular in Northern parts of India. Its normally made with mutton but this is a chicken version, and its just as good with chicken. I would suggest using some bone in pieces for the korma, but its a matter of choice and I know the lads in our family prefer the boneless variety, hence this version. When I saw this being made in India, I was shocked by the amount of clarified butter that was used, but I am a little stringent on the oil and I like to reserve butters for adding love at the end of the dish. Needless to say, when I am having a bad day, not much love is distributed in the form of butter.

Ingredients:
2 lbs boneless, skinless chicken breasts, cut into 1 inch cubes
2 cups greek yogurt, lightly whisked
2 large onions, thinly sliced
8 tbsp oil or clarified butter
3 inches piece of ginger, minced
6 cloves garlic, minced
4 fresh red chillies, minced
6 dried whole red chillies
2 tsp deghi mirch powder / kashmiri red powder (can be replaced with paprika powder)
1 tbsp coriander powder
¼ tsp turmeric powder
1 bay leaf
1 tsp cardamom powder
4 green cardamoms
1 tsp chicken masala
½ tsp clove powder
1 tsp freshly ground black pepper
salt to taste
¼ cup chicken stock
1 tbsp rose water

Method:
Heat 3 tbsp oil in a heavy base pan and saute the onions on medium heat. Sprinkle a little salt on the onions to expedite the process and cook until the onions soften and turn golden brown in colour. Blend these onions to a smooth paste, when they cool down add a tbsp of yogurt and set aside.

Marinate the chicken with all the powdered spices, the minced red chillies, the yogurt and a tbsp of oil. Leave to rest in the refrigerator for about an hour.

Heat 5 tbsp oil in a heavy base pan and saute the minced ginger, garlic, dried whole red chillies, the cardamoms and the bay leaf. Cook for a minute and add the marinated chicken. Stir in the chicken stock, reduce the heat and cover the pot. Let the chicken simmer on low heat for about half an hour.

Stir in the onion paste and sprinkle the fresh coriander leaves in there. I like to add a tbsp of crushed dried fenugreek leaves as they add a little zing of extra flavour. Cover the lid again and let it simmer for a further 5 minutes.

If you wish to add some extra love, then a big dollop of clarified butter does the trick.

Chicken Tikka Masala - British style
An all time favourite dish all over the world

Ingredients:
2 lbs boneless, skinless chicken breasts, cut into 1 inch cubes
2 medium onions, finely chopped
2 inch piece of ginger, minced
4 cloves of garlic, minced
1 green chilli, minced
1 tbsp sugar
1 tsp freshly ground black pepper
1 tsp red chilli powder (adjust to taste)
1 tbsp tandoori masala
1 tsp garam masala
A small bunch of fresh coriander leaves, finely chopped
1 tbsp dried fenugreek leaves
2 cups natural yogurt, lightly whisked
½ cup thick heavy cream (or 1 cup crème fraiche)
½ cup cashew nuts
1 tbsp tomato puree or paste
½ tsp red food colour (optional)
1 tsp turmeric powder
3 tbsp oil
1 can chopped tomatoes or 4 fresh plum tomatoes
1 tsp cumin seeds
1½ tsp coriander powder
1 cup chicken stock
salt to taste

Method:
In a zip loc bag, add 1 cup yogurt, the tandoori masala, ½ of the ginger paste, a pinch of salt, the freshly ground black pepper and the tomato puree. Mix well by massaging the bag from the outside and add the chicken pieces. Massage the pieces well into the marinade and leave to rest in the refrigerator overnight or for a minimum of 5-6 hours.

Lightly dry roast the cashew nuts on a skillet (do not brown then), let them cool before blending the cashewnuts with a little bit of water to make a thick smooth paste.

Heat oil in a medium sized pan, and add the cumin seeds. Fry for 10 seconds before adding in the onions, ginger and green chilli. Saute the onions till soft and light golden in colour. Stir in the garlic followed by all the spices. Add the tomatoes, tomato puree and the chicken stock. Use a hand blender and blitz to a smooth puree.

Stir in the food colour and the sugar, followed by the marinated chicken. Reduce the heat, cover the pot and let the chicken simmer for 20 minutes until fully cooked. Check half way in case you need to add more chicken stock or water.

Once the chicken is cooked, stir in the cashew nuts paste and the cream. Sprinkle some fresh coriander leaves and crushed dried fenugreek leaves. Mix well, cover the pot again and allow to simmer for a couple of minutes before switching off the heat but leaving the pot covered until ready to use.

Serve garnished with a little more cream, fresh coriander leaves and crispy fried onions.

Lahori Chicken and Chickpeas

Lahore is famous for many dishes, and the Chicken and chickpeas is famour for its creamy melt in your mouth texture. Its a Sunday brunch special dish served with freshly baked naans or kulchas. I am using canned chick peas for their convenience.

Ingredients:
½ cup red lentils, soaked in a cup of water for half an hour
2 16oz cans of chick peas, drained and washed
2 tbsp clarified butter
½ tsp cinnamon powder
2 lbs boneless, skinless chicken breasts, cut into 1 inch cubes
2 medium size onions, minced
2 inch piece of ginger, minced
4 cloves garlic, minced
4 green chillies, minced
1 tbsp cumin seeds
1 tsp turmeric powder
1 tbsp coriander powder
4 tbsp dried fenugreek leaves
1 tsp red chilli powder (adjust to taste)
1 cup greek yogurt, lightly whisked
1 bunch fresh coriander leaves, finely chopped
1 tsp freshly ground black pepper
1 tbsp chicken masala
1 tbsp chaat masala
1 cup chicken stock

Method:
Marinate the chicken with the onions, ginger, garlic, green chillies and a little salt for about half an hour.

Heat oil in a deep pot (or a dutch oven), add the cumin seeds and the cinnamon stick. Add the marinated chicken, the soaked red lentils (without the water), turmeric, salt, chicken stock and the yogurt. Mix well, reduce the heat, cover the pot and let the chicken simmer on low heat for about 10-15 minutes.

Stir in all the remaining ingredients, including the chick peas and the spices. You may need to add another cup of chicken stock or water, if there isn't enough gravy. Let the chicken simmer for a further 15-20 minutes until tender and stir in 2 tbsp of clarified butter for added flavour and love.

The best way to serve this dish is, to heat up 2-4 tbsp of clarified butter, add a pinch of cumin seeds, a couple of green chillies slit lengthways and once this starts to sizzle pour it over the chicken and chickpeas. Sprinkle some fresh coriander leaves and serve with a freshly baked naan or kulcha.

Mum's Chicken Curry

This is one of my mum's special curry, its simple to make and absolutely delicious. Mum likes to make the curry with bone-in pieces, and she now mixes half boneless chicken to accommodate everyone's tastes.

Ingredients:
3 lbs boneless, skinless chicken pieces
3 medium onions, thinly sliced
3 tbsp oil
2 inch piece of fresh ginger, grated
5 cloves of garlic, minced
4 tomatoes or 1 can of chopped plum tomatoes, minced
2 fresh green chillies (adjust to taste), minced
1 tsp turmeric powder
Small bunch fresh coriander leaves, finely chopped
1 batch chicken masala (see page 102)
½ tsp red chilli powder (optional)
2 cups chicken stock or water

Method:
Heat oil in large pot on medium heat and sauté the onions until soft and golden in colour. Add the ginger and green chillies and continue cooking for another 3-4 minutes.

Stir in the garlic, let it cook for 30 minutes before adding in the tomatoes. Reduce the heat and cover the pan. Let this cook for 4-5 minutes.

Using a hand blender, puree the gravy before adding the chicken pieces. Increase the heat to medium, fold the chicken well into the gravy and cover the pot. Let this cook for 5 minutes and stir in the chicken masala powder.

Add the chicken stock, cover the pot and let the chicken cook on low/ medium heat for 20 minutes. If gravy is too thick, add a cup of water.

Stir in the fresh coriander leaves. Serve hot with some boiled basmati rice and salad.

Chicken Koftas in a Creamy Rich Sauce
(without the cream) Page 62

Methi Chicken

Methi Chicken

Chicken cooked with fenugreek leaves. A Sunday brunch favourite that's finger licking good. However, the fenugreek leaves tend to have a slight bitter flavour that takes a little getting used to if you haven't tasted a fresh fenugreek dish before. One things for sure, there are never any leftovers.
Fresh fenugreek leaves can be easily found at most Indian grocery stores.

Ingredients:
2lbs boneless, skinless chicken pieces, cut into 1 inch cubes
2 large onions, thinly sliced
3 tomatoes, minced
1 tbsp tomato puree/ paste
1 cup heavy cream
1 cup greek yogurt, lightly whisked
5 green chillies, deseeded and minced
1 inch piece ginger, minced
2 cloves garlic, minced
2 small bunches of fresh fenugreek leaves, finely chopped
4 tbsp oil
1 tsp turmeric powder
1 tsp garam masala
1 tbsp cumin coriander powder
salt to taste
1 cup chicken stock

Method:
Marinate the chicken with the yogurt for a couple of hours.

Heat oil in a heavy based pot (or a dutch oven) and add the onions. Saute the onions till they are golden brown in colour and have softened. Stir in the minced ginger, garlic, green chilli and continue cooking for another couple of minutes, stirring continuously.

Stir in the tomatoes, the tomato paste and all the spices. Add a couple of tablespoons of the chicken stock and cook for 3-4 minutes, before adding the fenugreek leaves. Stir well and stir fry for a few minutes.

Once the fenugreek has softened and blended well with the onion mixture, add the marinated chicken. Stir well and add the remaining chicken stock. Cover the pot, reduce the heat and allow to simmer for 25-30 minutes.

Stir in the cream and cook on medium heat, stirring almost continuously to dry up the juices a little.

If the fenugreek feels a little bitter to taste, add a little bit more cream or butter, as it helps to take away the bitter flavour. Serve with some fresh naan bread or paranthas.

Kolhapuri Chicken
Hot and spicy, with very strong garlic flavours.

2lb boneless, skinless chicken breasts, cut into 1 inch cubes

Marinade:
1 tbsp chicken masala
1 tbsp ginger paste
1 tbsp garlic paste
Juice and rind of 1 lemon
1 tsp turmeric powder
1 tbsp red chilli powder

Gravy:
3 tbsp oil
2 tbsp chicken masala
1 tsp cumin seeds
2 medium onions
1 tsp coriander powder
4 fresh green chillies, finely chopped
2 tbsp garlic paste
2 tbsp white sesame seeds
2 tbsp white poppy seeds
1 can coconut milk
½ can chopped tomatoes or 2 medium size fresh tomatoes
a bunch of fresh coriander leaves, finely chopped

Method:
In a large zip loc bag, combine the chicken with the marinating spices. Leave to marinate in fridge for at least 2 hours.

Heat oil in a medium size pot, add the cumin seeds and fry them for 30 seconds before stirring in the onions. Saute the onions until soft and light golden in colour. Add the green chillies and cook for another minute.

Lower the heat and add the garlic following by the sesame seeds and the poppy seeds. Stir well and cook for 2-3 minutes on low heat.

Add the chicken masala and the coriander masala, stir well before adding the tomatoes. Increase the heat to medium and continue cooking, stirring occasionally. Cook for 5 minutes and remove from heat.

Using a hand blender or a food blender, puree the sauce and return to cook on the pot. Stir in half the can of coconut milk and add the marinated chicken to the pot. Mix well.

Reduce the heat to low, stir in the remaining coconut milk, cover the pot and let the chicken cook for 20-25 minutes or until cooked through. Once the chicken is cooked, stir in the fresh coriander leaves.

Garnish with fried curry leaves before serving on a bed of basmati rice.

Chicken Changezi

A fantastic rich gravy made with lots of onions, tomatoes and spices. Theres lots of different steps to this recipe, but it gives amazing results. I like to use chicken legs and thighs for this recipe, together with some boneless pieces. The puffed lotus seeds are easily available at Indian grocery stores.

Ingredients:
2lbs boneless, skinless chicken pieces, cut into 1 inch cubes
1 boiled egg
3 large onions, finely chopped
1 cup cashewnuts
8 tbsp clarified butter / oil + more for deep frying
1 cup whole milk
2 inch piece of ginger, minced
5 cloves garlic, minced
4 tbsp tomato puree/ paste
4 tomatoes, finely chopped or 1 can of crushed/diced tomatoes
1 tbsp coriander powder
1 tsp red chilli powder
6 green chillies, finely chopped
1 tsp chicken masala
1 tsp garam masala
1 cup heavy cream
2 tsp chaat masala
3 tbsp lemon juice
1 tbsp dried fenugreek leaves
20 makhane / puffed lotus seeds, fried in oil
salt to taste
1 cup chicken stock

Method:
Heat 4 tbsp oil in a pan and saute the onions until light golden in colour. Add the cashewnuts to the onions, and continue cooking for a further few minutes until the onions turn a darker golden brown. Let the onions cool a little before blending the onions and cashewnuts to a paste. If its too dry, use some of the chicken stock.

Deep fry the puffed lotus seeds and keep aside.

Heat 4 tbsp oil in a pot and saute the ginger, garlic, green chillies for a minute before adding all the spices and the tomatoes. Stir in the milk, followed by the chicken and the chicken stock. Reduce the heat, cover the pot and allow to simmer on low heat for 20-25 minutes.

Add the onion cashew paste, the fenugreek leaves, the cream and the fried puffed lotus seeds. Cover the pot and let it simmer for another 15 minutes on low heat.

Garnish with finely chopped green chillies and boiled egg sliced into quarters.

Tandoori Chicken Jalfrezi

A quick and easy dish and its perfect for when you have unexpected guests or you just don't want to spend hours in the kitchen. As the name suggests, its a Tandoori Chicken stir fry

Ingredients:
chicken tikka boti (recipe on page 29)
2 inch piece of ginger, cut into julienne strips
2 green chillies, finely chopped
6 cloves garlic, minced
1 large green pepper/ capsicum, cut into 1 inch cubes
1 medium size red onion, sliced
8 button mushrooms, quartered
½ cup chicken stock
2 tbsp chicken masala
2 tbsp tomato puree/ paste
1 tsp freshly ground black pepper
salt to taste
3 tbsp oil

Method:
Heat oil in a wok and saute the onions, ginger, garlic and green chillies. Cook until the onions have softened and they are golden in colour.

Stir in the spices and the tomato paste, as well as the chicken stock. Stir well and add the chicken.

Continue cooking on medium heat until the gravy thickens a bit.

Serve sprinkled with some fresh coriander leaves and some saffron rice.

Malabar Chicken Korma

A slightly spicy traditional South Indian korma made with creamy coconut. Traditionally this dish is made using Chicken thighs and potatoes, it is a bit of a fussy recipe but worth the extra work. Don't be intimidated by the long list of ingredients.

Ingredients:
3 lbs chicken thighs (skins removed but bone-in), halved through the bone
1½ lb baby potatoes, peeled with a couple of slits made on both sides, soaked in cold water
½ cup cashew nuts
½ cup unsweetened dessicated coconut
2 medium onions, finely chopped
1 large onion, thinly sliced
2-4 green chillies (adjust to taste), minced
½ tsp lemon juice
2 inch piece of fresh ginger or 1 tbsp ginger paste
4 cloves garlic, minced
1 tsp tomato paste
4 green cardamoms
2 bay leaf
4 tsp cumin powder
6 tbsp oil
4 tsp coriander seeds
20 curry leaves
1 can unsweetened coconut milk
2 tsp fennel powder
1 tsp kashmiri red chilli powder (can be replaced by paprika if not available)
1 tsp red chilli powder
4 dried whole red chillies
1 tsp freshly ground black pepper
A small bunch of fresh coriander leaves
1 can chopped tomatoes or 4 fresh plum tomatoes, finely chopped
Salt to taste
2 tsp turmeric powder
1 cup chicken stock

In a zip loc bag, marinate the chilcken with salt, ½ of the turmeric powder, kashmiri red chilli powder, red chilli powder and the lemon juice. Massage the spices into the chicken well and leave in refrigerator for at least 3 hours, or preferably overnight.

Blend the cashews together into a smooth paste using a little bit of water, and combine with ½ of the can of coconut milk, and set aside.

In a large pot, heat 3 tbsp of oil, add the onions followed by the curry leaves, bay leaves and a pinch of salt. Fry these until the onions are golden brown in colour before adding the green chillies, the dried red chillies, ginger, garlic, coriander seeds and the dessicated coconut. Fry until the coconut becomes golden brown, stirring continuously.

Mindfully Spiced Chicken • Page 81

Let the gravy base cool for a few minutes before adding a little water to this and grind to a smooth paste. Heat the remaining oil in a pan and add the onions. Cook until the onions are crispy fried to a dark golden brown colour before adding in the tomatoes followed by the tomato paste. When the tomatoes soften and mix in well with the onions, add the ground paste mixture to these onions and stir well. Add salt and the remaining spices to this mixture along with ½ a cup of water. Stir well.

Add the chicken to the gravy and stir well, making sure the chicken pieces are coated well. Add the potatoes with ½ the can of coconut milk and the chicken stock. Reduce the heat, cover the pot and let it simmer for about 20-25 minutes or until the chicken and the potatoes are cooked through.

Stir in the remaining coconut milk that had been combined with the cashew paste, and cook for a further minutes cover on low heat. Stir every minute to check the gravy has been thickened by the cashew paste and you have the required consistency.

This Korma is best made a few hours ahead, so you just need to reheat on medium heat before serving. Serve hot garnished with fried curry leaves and some fresh coriander leaves.

Chicken Vindaloo

One of the spiciest curries and ever so popular at most Indian restaurants. This is my take on the traditional Anglo-Indian recipe.

2 lbs boneless, skinless chicken breasts, cut into 1 inch cubes

Marinade:
1 tbsp cumin coriander powder
1 tsp turmeric powder
2 tsp chicken masala
¼ tsp ground cinnamon
2 tsp mustard powder
1 tsp red chilli powder
2 inch piece of ginger, minced
3 tbsp white wine vinegar
2 tsp sugar
salt to taste
3 green chillies, minced

Gravy:
4 tbsp oil
8 garlic cloves, minced
2 medium size onions, thinly sliced
4 red chillies, chopped finely (adjust to taste)
1 lb tomatoes, finely chopped or 2 cans of crushed / diced tomatoes
3 tbsp tomato puree/ paste
2 tsp kashmiri red chilli powder (or paprika)
4 dried red chillies
1 can coconut milk
4-6 curry leaves
1 red pepper / capsicum, thinly sliced
salt to taste
1 cup chicken stock

Method:
Marinate the chicken in a ziploc bag with all the ingredients for the marinade. Massage the chicken from outside the bag to help blend the spices well into the chicken. Leave to rest overnight in the fridge.

Heat oil in a large pot and add the onions and the curry leaves. Saute until the onions are golden in colour before stirring in the red pepper followed by all the spices and the tomatoes. Cook on medium high for 5 minutes, stirring from time to time.

Add the marinated chicken and the chicken stock. Reduce the heat, cover the pot and allow to simmer for 20-25 minutes until the chicken is fully cooked. Stir in the coconut milk, and let the chicken cook for a final 5 minutes before serving with a bowl of basmati rice.

Chicken Korma- British style

This book would not be complete without the British version of the Chicken Korma. Its a very mildly spiced Korma, very creamy and absolutely loved by children.

Ingredients
2 lbs boneless, skinless chicken breasts, cut into 1 inch cubes
1 large onion, minced
1 can coconut milk
1 cup heavy full fat cream
1 cup greek yogurt
2 cups chicken stock
1 tsp turmeric powder
4 tbsp oil
2 tomatoes, finely chopped or ½ can of crushed/ diced tomatoes
1 inch piece of ginger, minced
3 cloves of garlic, minced
½ tsp ground cumin
a pinch of nutmeg, freshly ground
a pinch of cinnamon powder
freshly ground black pepper to taste
salt to taste
a handful of fresh coriander leaves, finely chopped

Method
Heat oil in a pan and saute the onions until they have turned golden brown in colour. Add the ginger and garlic and continue cooking for a minute before adding in all the dry spices, followed by the tomatoes.

Add the chicken pieces and a little of the chicken stock, and cook for a couple of minutes before adding teh remaining stock. Cover the pan, and simmer on low heat for 15-20 minutes or until the chicken is cooked through.

Add the cream, the cononut milk as well as the yogurt. Stir well and simmer for a further 5 minutes before serving.

Serve garnished with fresh coriander leaves and coconut flakes.

Papaji's Butter Chicken

This is the traditional Butter Chicken that my grandad introduced me to, and one that I tasted at the original Moti Mahal, in Old Delhi. Its difficult to replicate the exact flavour with modern ingredients, but this is as close as I can make it. I wish I had had the opportunity of actually cooking this recipe for my grandfather before he passed away, but I think of him as I write this recipe. I'm sure he would have been proud.

Ingredients:
1 tandoori roast chicken legs (recipe page 56)
2 lbs fresh tomatoes, skins removed and pureed in a food processor
4 tbsp tomato puree
4 tbsp oil
1 large onion, finely chopped
2 inch piece of ginger, minced
6 cloves of garlic, minced
14 cashewnuts, lightly dry roasted and blended to a paste using some water
1 bay leaf
1 tbsp cumin coriander powder
1 tbsp dried fenugreek leaves
3-4 green chillies, minced (adjust to taste)
1 tbsp kashmiri chilli powder (or paprika if not available)
1 tbsp chicken masala
1 cup heavy full fat cream
½ cup butter
a handful of fresh coriander leaves, finely chopped
salt and freshly ground black pepper to taste
½ cup chicken stock

Method:
Heat oil in a large pot and add the onions. Saute for a few minutes, until the onions have softened and are a light golden in colour. Add the ginger, garlic, green chillies and the bay leaf. Continue cooking for a further 2-3 minutes.

Add all the spices followed by the tomatoes and the chicken stock. Reduce the heat and let the sauce simmer on low for 10-15 minutes.

Using a hand blender, blitz the sauce into a smooth puree and strain the sauce. Return the strained sauce into the pot along with the tandoori roast chicken. Sprinkle the dried fenugreek leaves and the coriander leaves into the sauce, and also stir in the butter and the cream.

Cover the pot, and simmer for 5 minutes before serving the butter chicken with a freshly baked naan. This butter chicken tastes even nicer the following day, but it rarely lasts that long.

Serve with a dollop of butter as well as some cream on top of the butter chicken, and sprinkled with some fresh coriander leaves.

Jakey's Butter Chicken

I was introduced to the Canadian version of Butter Chicken when I came to Canada. I was surprised at how different the flavours and spices were, in comparison to what I was used to. This is my version of the Canadian Butter Chicken and I have to say, it has quite a big following since I first made it at Crossroads market. Its simple, easy and delicately spiced. If you like the spicy version as I do, add some extra minced green chillies, and as all butter chickens it tastes better the next day!

Ingredients:
2 lbs boneless, skinless chicken breasts, cut into 1 inch cubes
2 tbsp flour
2 tbsp butter
1 cup heavy full fat cream / whipping cream
4 tbsp dried fenugreek leaves, crushed by hand and stems removed
2 cups chicken stock
8 fresh tomatoes, minced or 1 can of crushed tomatoes
2 tbsp tomato puree
1 tsp sugar
1 tbsp cumin coriander powder
1 tbsp ginger powder
1 tbsp chicken masala
1 tbsp tandoori masala
1 tsp white pepper
2 tbsp onion powder
1 tsp chaat masala
1 tsp turmeric powder
1 tbsp tomato ketchup
4 drops of red icing colour
salt to taste

Method:
Heat the butter and add the flour to make a roux. Slowly add a little bit of the chicken stop whilst stirring the rou with the other hand.

Stir in all the spices, the sugar, the cream and the remaining chicken stock. Add the tomatoes and the chicken. Bring the sauce to a boil, cover the pot, reduce the heat and let it simmer for 15-20 minutes until the chicken has cooked through. Stir in a tbsp of the tomato ketchup and let the butter chicken rest for a few minutes before serving.

Serve on a bed of saffron rice and drizzle some extra cream on top, as well as some fresh coriander leaves.

Jakey's Butter Chicken

Raj's Yogurt Chicken

Rajs Yogurt Chicken

One of my mum's recipes adored by my brother in law, Raj. My mum's version has 'invisible' ginger and onions, as she liquidises the spices before adding them to the Chicken as Raj does not like to bite into whole spices. This dish is spicy enough to clear your sinuses and the tangy flavour from the yogurt is amazing and goes fantastically with some rice. We had some Mango kulfi after testing this recipe as we accidentally spiced up the dish twice.
My mum's recipe doesn't use as much yogurt or spice, but this is my spin on it.

Ingredients:
1 lb boneless chicken
1 medium size onion, finely chopped
1 tsp cumin seeds
2 inch piece of ginger, finely chopped
6 cloves garlic, minced
1 tbsp dried fenugreek leaves
Salt and freshly ground pepper to taste
1 tsp red chilli powder
1 tbsp chicken masala
1 tsp garam masala
4 green chillies (adjust to taste), finely chopped
3 cups natural yogurt
a handful of fresh coriander leaves, finely chopped

Method:
Heat oil in a pot and saute the onions, ginger, green chillies and the garlic, until the onions have softened and are golden brown in colour.

Add all the spices, followed by the chicken and the yogurt. Mix well, cover the pot, reduce the heat and simmer for 30 minutes or until the chicken is fully cooked.

Serve garnished with fresh coriander leaves.

Variation:
Once the onions have been cooked in oil, transfer the entire ingredients into a slow cooker.
It cooks beautifully!

Quick Chicken Pulao

I freeze a lot of my curries, specially the ones that have the rich gravy base in 1 cup portions in freezer bags, just to be able to make the instant pulao.

Ingredients:
1 cup Chicken Changezi (for recipe see page 77)
1 small onion, thinly sliced
1 green chilli (optional), finely chopped
1 star aniseed
1 tbsp cumin seeds
2-3 cloves
2 cups basmati rice
2 cups chicken stock
salt to taste
2 tbsp oil

Method:
Heat oil in a large pot and add the cumin seeds. Cook until they start to sizzle and stir in the onions and green chillies. Saute until the onions are a darker shade of golden brown before stirring in the Chicken Changezi.

Add all the remaining ingredients, including the rice and the chicken stock and also add a further 1 ½ cups of water. Bring to a boil, and cover the pot. Lower the heat to the minimum and allow the rice to cook on low heat for about 15 minutes or until you smell the aroma of cooked basmati rice.

Switch off the heat, check to see if the rice are done. Since
basmati rice qualities tends to be different everywhere, its a little hard to gauge how long exactly it will take to cook the rice perfectly. If the rice feel very soft then remove the lid and give them a little stirring up to put some cold air in there for the steam to escape. If the rice feel like they need a litle bit more time, then just put the lid back on and let the steam inside the rice do its job for the next 5 minutes.

Serve the instant biryani with a nice refreshing raita and a bit of salad for the perfect lunch or dinner made within minutes.

Non-Traditional Chicken

Chicken Meatloaf

Spicy Stilton Chicken Burgers

Spicy Garlic Chicken

Sweet & Spicy Sesame Chicken

Ginger Chicken

Chilli Chicken

Chicken Manchurian

Chicken Hakka Noodles

Gamenight Chicken Pizza

Chicken Meatloaf

When we were testing this recipe, I completely forgot to grease the pan and the result is as shown on page 89! This is a delicately spiced meatloaf and the combination of the sweet and crunchy edging with the spicy juicy meatloaf is irresistible with a dollop of Tomato ketchup.

Ingredients:
½ lb minced chicken
1 large onion, finely chopped
1 tbsp cumin seeds
1 courgette, grated with the skin on
salt and pepper to taste
½ tsp red chilli powder
2 green chillies, minced (adjust to taste)
½ tsp ginger powder
1 tsp garlic paste
2 tomatoes, finely chopped
1 cup breadcrumbs
1 egg
1 tbsp oil + more for greasing the baking sheet

Basting:
Coriander Oil
3 tbsp tomato ketchup

Method:
Preheat the oven to 350F / 180C / Gas mark 4. Grease a baking sheet or tray and keep aside.

Combine all the ingredients together in a large bowl. Grease your hands with a little oil, and just knead the mix together, until it forms a smooth dough. Place the mixture onto the baking sheet and shape into a loaf.

Baste the meatloaf with some coriander oil and then brush some tomato ketchup on top of the loaf. Bake in oven for at least 1 hour, until cooked through.

Serve with some mashed potatoes and a spicy gravy sauce.

Spicy Stilton Chicken Burgers

Ingredients:
1 lb minced chicken
1 egg, lightly beaten
¼ cup stilton cheese, crumbled
1 tbsp sriracha hot sauce
½ cup fresh breadcrumbs
salt, freshly ground black pepper to taste
1 tsp red chilli powder (adjust to taste)
1 tbsp red chilli flakes (adjust to taste)
½ tsp curry powder

Method:
Combine everything really well in a bowl. Form four 3/4 inch thick patties.

Grill the patties over medium high heat on the BBQ for about 5 minutes each side of until cooked through. Alternatively, cook in a preheated oven at 375F / 190C / Gas Mark 5 for about 15-20 minutes until cooked through.

Serve in a soft burger bun with a slice of tomato and red onions.

Spicy Garlic Chicken

Makes amazing sandwiches, paninis and great with Salad in the summer.
Ingredients:
4 boneless, skinless chicken breasts
2 tbsp olive oil
1 tbsp. red chilli flakes (adjust to taste)
3 cloves garlic, crushed and finely chopped
1 tsp onion powder
1 tsp dried coriander flakes
½ tsp freshly ground black pepper
2 tsp sweet chilli sauce

Method:
Mix all the dry ingredients together before mixing in the oil and the chilli flakes. Make a couple of slits on the thickest parts of the chicken breasts and place them in a zip lock bag. Pour the spicy garlic marinate and refrigerate for at least an hour before cooking.

Preheat oven to 375F / 190C / Gas Mark 5 and cook the chicken on a lightly greased baking sheet for 20-25 minutes or until the chicken is fully cooked through. Serve on a bed of salad or with rice.

Sweet and Spicy Sesame Chicken
A popular Hakka Chinese dish

Ingredients:
2 lbs boneless, skinless chicken breasts, cut into 1 inch cubes
2 tbsp brown sesame seeds
2 cloves garlic, crushed and finely chopped
2 tbsp mushroom soy sauce
1 tbsp honey
2 tbsp sweet chilli sauce
½ tsp red chilli powder (adjust to taste)
1 green chilli, deseeded and finely chopped (adjust to taste)
2 egg whites
½ cup corn starch
1 tbsp sesame oil
1 tbsp cooking oil
½ tsp freshly ground black pepper
1 large onion, sliced very thinly

Method:
Lightly roast the sesame seeds on a dry pan or skillet. Let them cool before cooking.
Combine the sesame seeds with soy sauce, honey, sweet chilli sauce and set aside. Make a paste using the corn starch, the red chilli powder, salt, black pepper and the egg whites. Marinate chicken in this paste for at least 20-30 minutes in the refrigerator before cooking.

Heat the two oils in a large work or pan and sauté the onions and green chillies until they soften and the onions are translucent in colour. Add the chicken strips and stir fry until the chicken is fully cooked and turns a soft golden colour. Remove from heat and stir in the sauce mix.

Toss well and garnish with freshly chopped coriander, some green onions and some lightly roasted white sesame seeds before serving on a bed of fragrant rice or hakka noodles.

Ginger Chicken
Hot and spicy – influenced by Hakka Chinese cuisine

Ingredients:
2 lbs boneless, skinless chicken breasts, cut into cubes
1 tbsp ginger paste
2 inch piece of fresh ginger, cut into thin julienne strips
juice and rind of 1 lemon
1 tsp red chilli powder
1 egg white
2 tbsp corn starch
4 fresh green chillies, finely chopped
2 medium size onions (red onions preferred), cut into cubes
1 tsp dark soy sauce
4 green onions with stalks, finely chopped
1 tbsp tabasco sauce
oil to deep fry + 2 tbsp
salt to taste

Method:
Using a spoonful of cold water make a paste using the corn starch, and set aside. Slit the green chillies lengthways and deseed if you don't want too much heat.

In a large zip loc bag combine the chicken with ginger paste, lemon juice and rind, salt, red chilli powder and mix well. Let marinate for at least 30 minutes. Add egg and half of the cornstarch paste and rub into the chicken well.

Deep fry the chicken pieces on medium heat. Discard any excess marinade. In a work or large skillet, heat the 2 tbsp of oil and fry the green chillies and the julienned ginger slices. Add the onions and sauté till they start to soften. Add the soya sauce, tabasco sauce, the remaining half of the cornstarch paste stirring continuously.

Add ½ a cup of water and blend in well. Add the fried chicken and toss well, adding the green onion to the chicken. Serve hot with rice or hakka noodles.

Chilli Chicken

Ingredients:
2 lbs boneless, skinless chicken breasts, cut into 1 inch cubes
4 green peppers, cut into 1 inch cubes
2 large onions, cut into 1 inch cubes
4 inch piece of fresh ginger, cut into julienne strips
4-6 fresh green chillies (adjust to taste), finely chopped
A large bunch of fresh coriander leaves, finely chopped
3 tbsp dark soy sauce
1 tbsp Worcestershire sauce
1 tbsp tabasco sauce
1 tbsp fine granulated sugar
3 tbsp corn starch
4 tbsp oil
1 tsp lemon juice

Method:
Combine the 3 sauces, the sugar and the corn starch paste, and set aside.

In a zip loc bag, marinate the chicken with 2 tbsp corn starch, a pinch of salt and lemon juice. Rub and massage the chicken well and set aside. This does not need to be marinated for very long.

Heat half the oil in a large pan or wok, and add the ginger. Stir fry for a minute before adding the green chillies. Stir again and add the chicken. Stir fry the chicken for a couple of minutes, then reduce the heat and add 1 cup of water. Cover and let it simmer for 10-15 minutes until the chicken is no longer raw.

In the meantime, take another pan and heat the remaining oil and stir fry the onions for a couple of minutes before adding the green peppers. Stir fry both until they are softer and the onions are light golden in colour. Combine with the chicken. Stir in the sauce mix that had been set aside and mix well. Continue cooking the chicken for a couple of minutes stirring continuously and the gravy should start to thicken.

Sprinkle some salt, but be weary as the soy sauce and worcestershire sauce both contain salt. Cover and remove from heat. Serve hot garnished with fresh coriander leaves.

Chicken Manchurian

I love the Delhi flavour of Chicken Manchurian with nice spicy Hakka noodles, and its something I order every time I visit there.

1lb boneless, skinless chicken breasts, cut into 1inch cubes

Marination:
1 egg, lightly whisked
1 tbsp flour
1 tbsp oil,
salt and freshly ground black pepper to taste
2 cloves of garlic, minced
oil for deep frying

Gravy:
4 cloves of garlic, minced
4 tbsp ketchup
4 tbsp chilli garlic sauce
1 green pepper, cubed into the same size as the chicken
1 onion, finely chopped
juice and zest from 1 medium sized lemon
4 pineapple slices or 1 small can of pineapple bits
2 tbsp worcestershire sauce
2 tbsp corn flour mixed with 2 tbsp of water to form a paste
3-4 tbsp vegetable oil
2 cups water
Salt and freshly ground black pepper to taste

Method:
Add all the marinating ingredients into a zip lock bag and add the chicken cubes. Massage gently from outside the bag and place in the refrigerator to marinate for at least 2 hours.

Heat the oil to 360F and deep fry the chicken until golden brown and cooked through. I like to take one piece out first, usually the biggest piece is there is and I slice it open to check the piece is not pink. If the biggest piece is done, the remaining pieces should technically be done too.

Remove and place on paper towels or spread them on a wire rack placed over a baking sheet (helps keep them crisp), whilst you work through the gravy.

In a large pan, heat 3-4 tbsp of vegetable oil over medium high heat and saute the onions until soft and translucent, add the garlic and the chopped peppers. Continue to stir fry for 3 minutes and then add the pineapple chunks. After another 2 minutes of frying, add the remaining spices along with the chilli garlic sauce, ketchup, worcestershire sauce and two cups of water. Stir these thoroughly before adding the corn flour paste. Let the gravy simmer continuously until it thickens.

Add a slice of a lemon wedge before serving on a bed of rice.

Chicken Hakka Noodles
Very popular street food in Delhi, and one of my absolute favourites

Ingredients:
1 lb boneless, skinless chicken pieces, cut into thin strips
1 large onion, thinly sliced
1 green pepper / capsicum, thinly sliced
1 cup shredded cabbage
2 carrot, cut into thin julienne strips
1 egg, lightly whisked
500g packet of chicken chowmein noodles
1 tsp dark soy sauce
1 tbsp mushroom soy sauce
1 tbsp white vinegar
1 tbsp sriracha hot sauce
2 green chillies, finely chopped
1 tbsp tomato ketchup
1 tbsp of sweet chilli garlic sauce (optional)
2 inch piece of ginger, cut into thin julienne strips
salt and black pepper
5 tbsp oil

Method:
Get all the ingredients ready and within arms reach as this dish will cook quite quickly and things move pretty fast once you are stir frying on high heat. Mix all the sauces together and set aside.

Boil the chicken chowmein noodles as per packet instructions, but leave them a little crisp than normal and drain them in cold running water. Separate with a fork and set aside.

Cook the egg as a very thin omelette, almost like a crepe. Let it cool, roll up and cut into thin long strips.

Heat the oil in a wok on high heat and add the ginger and the green chillies. Stir fry and add the onions. Keep stirring continuously and cook until the onions soften and turn translucent in colour. Add the chicken strips and cook until the chicken is fully cooked. Add the carrots, cabbage and the green pepper and continue stir frying at high heat.

Stir in the sauces followed by the noodles. Keep stirring continuously until all the noodles are coated well and its nice to get a few of them extra crispy for that proper street vendor flavour.

Serve garnished with the egg strips on top and spicy chutney on the side. These noodles are delicious on their own or served with any of the hakka influenced dishes.

Gamenight Chicken Pizza

I keep a stash of frozen pizza bases for days when I don't fancy making anything complicated. Its perfect for gamenight as it keeps the boys happy when they are having fun and it gives me more time to do whatever I may choose to do! Leftover chicken with fresh vegetables make this Pizza a hit everytime!

Ingredients:
10 or 12 inch store bought pizza base (or even a naan bread)
1 cup of Raj's yogurt chicken (page 87)
¼ red onion, thinly sliced
¼ green pepper / capsicum, thinly sliced
1 green chilli, deseeded and finely chopped (adjust to taste)
¼ cup mozzarella cheese (add more/less according to taste)

Method:
Preheat the oven to 400F / 200C/ Gas mark 6 and lightly grease a pizza baking tray.

To start assembling the pizza, spread the yogurt chicken at the base of the pizza. The gravy of the chicken works in place of the usual tomato base. If some of the chicken pieces are too big, cut them into smaller pieces before spreading them on the pizza.

Sprinkle the onions, green pepper, green chillies evenly all over the pizza followed by the mozzarella cheese. Bake for about 10 minutes, or until the pizza is cooked through.

Serve with a crispy salad and a bottle of beer!

(Picture shown on the back cover of this book)

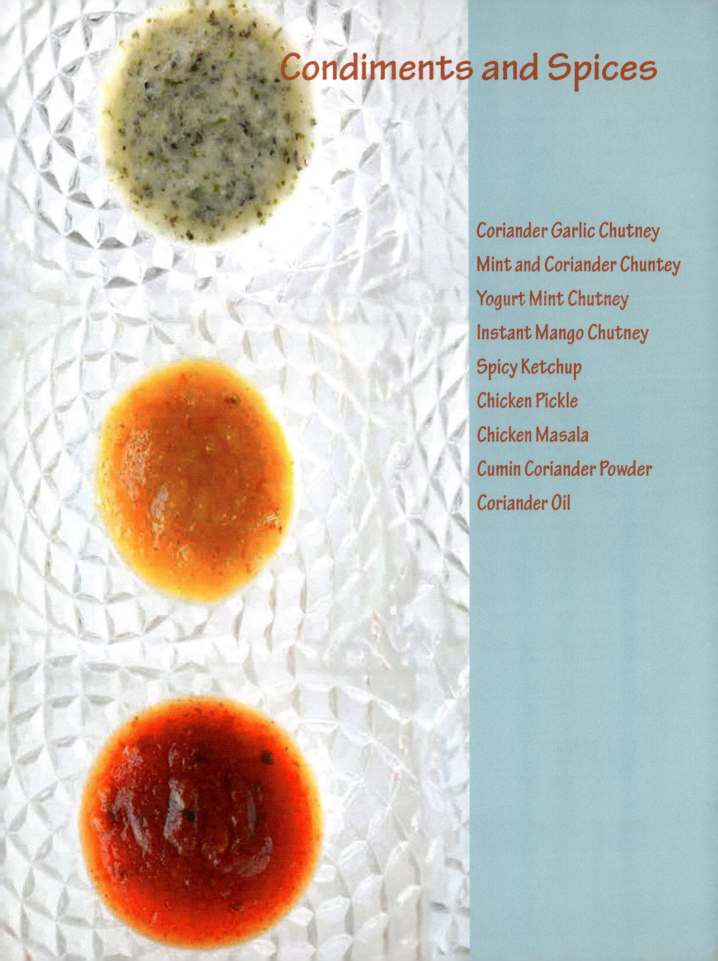

Condiments and Spices

Coriander Garlic Chutney

Mint and Coriander Chuntey

Yogurt Mint Chutney

Instant Mango Chutney

Spicy Ketchup

Chicken Pickle

Chicken Masala

Cumin Coriander Powder

Coriander Oil

Coriander Garlic Chutney

10 cloves of fresh garlic (if you can get green garlic, that would be perfect & include the greens)
1 bunch of fresh coriander, include the stems, roughly chopped
juice and rind of 1 lemon
1 tbsp chick pea flour
½ cup water
salt to taste

Method:
Dry roast the chick pea flour on a skillet, until it changes colour. Remove and let it cool.
Combine the ingredients and blitz in a blender until you have a smooth chutney. Keep refrigerated.

Mint and Coriander Chutney
My favourite sandwich spread!

2 bunches of fresh mint, hard stems removed, roughly chopped
1 bunch of fresh coriander leaves, include the stems, roughly chopped
1 medium size onion, roughly sliced
juice and rind of 1 lemon
1 tbsp sugar or honey
3-4 green chillies
salt to taste
1 tsp white vinegar (gives it longevity)
1 granny smith apple (optional)

Method:
Combine all the ingredients and blitz in a blender until you have a smooth chutney. Keep refrigerated.

Yogurt Mint Chutney

1 cup of yogurt, lightly whisked
3 tbsp mint and coriander chutney
salt to taste
freshly ground black pepper to taste
a pinch of chaat masala

Combine and keep refrigerated until ready to serve.

Instant Mango Chutney

½ cup mango pulp (canned)
3 tbsp mint and coriander chutney

Combine to make the fastest mango chutney in an instant.

Chicken Pickle

A North Indian specialty, and this recipe is our family recipe that has been handed down to me. This is a very spicy chicken pickle that keeps well for nearly 60 days but it never stays around for that long. I use it as a pizza topping, in my wraps, sandwiches and it tastes fantastic with a naan bread. It takes a little time to put together, but its worth the investment of time. My version is the boneless chicken version, but the real version has the bone-in chicken.

Ingredients:
2 lbs boneless, skinless chicken pieces, cut into 1 inch cubes
1 lb red onions, roughly chopped
6 cloves of garlic, halved
5 inch piece of ginger, roughly chopped
1 tbsp cinnamon powder
2 tbsp black peppercorns, crushed
1 nutmeg, grated
2 tbsp cloves, crushed
2 tbsp mace leaves, finely crushed
2 tbsp black cardamom seeds, finely crushed
1 litre mustard oil (available at all Indian grocers)
2 tbsp turmeric powder
25 green chillies, slit lengthways
2 cups white vinegar
2 tbsp red chilli powder
3 tbsp salt (adjust to taste)

Method:
Heat the oil in a large wide mouthed pot, and fry the garlic. Set aside to cool, and then grind to a paste. Repeat the same process with the ginger, the onions and then the chicken.

Traditionally the spices were kept whole in the pickle with some of them being crushed just to release the flavour, however since we have some fussy eaters in our family, I grind them all the spices to powder for this recipe. It doesn't affect the taste, and its much easier for me.

Heat the pot again that was used before, with the oil still in there and we re-fry the ground onions, ginger and garlic. Add the salt and the green chillies. Cook for a minute or so before adding the turmeric powder, red chilli powder and then turn the heat off. Stir in the vinegar, and there should be enough vinegar to cover everything in the pot. Whilst the heat is still off, add the chicken and stir well. Sprinkle all the remaining spices onto the chicken, stir well and switch the heat back on. Cover the chicken and allow to simmer on low heat for 3-5 minutes.

The pickle can be eaten whilst its fresh but it will get its real flavour after 5 days. Store in a sterilised jar, just as you would with other preserves and pickles, but this one will have to be stored in the refrigerator. If you make this in the summer, try to leave the jar out in the sun for 3-4 hours to expedite the natural pickling process.

Spicy Ketchup

1 cup tomato ketchup

½ cup chilli garlic sauce
4 tbsp sriracha sauce
1 tsp white vinegar

Combine to make a quick spicy ketchup that goes really well with the samosas and the chicken turnovers.

Chicken Masala
Makes one batch

Ingredients:
2 tbsp coriander seeds
1 tbsp cumin seeds
4 black cardamoms
4 green cardamoms
2 bay leaves
17 black peppercorns
1 stick cinnamon bark
1 star aniseed
1 tsp fennel seeds
1 tsp dried fenugreek leaves
1 tsp ginger powder
½ tsp salt
1 mace leaf
2 cloves

Method:
Break the cinnamon bark into 3-4 small pieces. Dry roast the coriander seeds, cumin and fennel seeds on low heat, stirring from time to time, until you can smell the fragrance of the spices. Set aside to cool down. On very low heat, warm the remaining ingredients in a dry pan for 30 seconds only. Remove from heat. In a spice or coffee grinder, grind all the spices along with the salt, until you have a coarse looking powder. This makes one batch of masala mix and ideally should be consumed within 6-8 weeks.

Cumin Coriander Powder

This spice mix is mentioned quite a bit through the book and I make this in large quantities as I use this in many recipes. Its a part of my everyday spice box.

1 cup coriander seeds
½ cup cumin seeds

Method:
Dry roast the seeds in a frying pan until the coriander seeds start to change colour a bit. Let them cool down before blitzing them through a coffee or spice grinder. Store in a container and this should ideally be consumed within 6-8 weeks.

Coriander oil

1 large bunch of coriander leaves, with stems, roughly chopped
1 cup olive oil
2-4 green chillies (adjust to taste)
1 tbsp salt

Method:
Blitz everything in a blender and store in a jar, in the refrigerator until ready to use.

INDEX

Almond Chicken Korma, 70
Arabic Chicken and Peach Salad, 21
BBQ Chicken Malai Boti Kebabs, 29
Black Pepper & Cumin Wings, 48
Burgers, Spicy Stilton Chicken, 94
Butter Chicken, Jakeys, 86
Butter Chicken, Papajis, 85
Cajun Mango Wings, 49
Chaap, Chicken, 66
Chaat, Dad's Chicken, 41
Changezi, Chicken, 79
Chapli Kebabs, 28
Chasni, Chicken, 61
Chettinadu Chicken, 64
Chicken 65, 42
Chicken and Mushroom Soup, 17
Chicken and Tomato Soup, 16
Chicken Chaap, 66
Chicken Changezi, 79
Chicken Chasni, 61
Chicken Dopiaza, 67
Chicken Hakka Noodles, 99
Chicken Jalfrezi, 69
Chicken Koftas in a creamy rich sauce, 62
Chicken Korma - British Style, 84
Chicken Korma - Delhi Style, 63
Chicken Manchurian, 98
Chicken Masala, 104
Chicken Pakora, 39, 40
Chicken Pickle, 103
Chicken Samosa, 27
Chicken Shashlik, 43
Chicken Shwarma, 33
Chicken Tikka Boti, 30
Chicken Tikka Masala - British Style, 72
Chicken Tikka Turnovers, 36
Chicken Vindaloo, 83
Chicken, Chilli, 97
Chicken, Ginger, 96
Chicken, Kolhapuri, 78
Chicken, Methi, 77
Chicken, Pumpkin, 65
Chicken, Raj's Yogurt, 89
Chicken, Spicy Garlic, 94
Chicken, Spinach, 68
Chicken, Sweet and Spicy Sesame, 95
Chickpeas, Lahori Chicken, 73
Chilli Chicken, 97
Chutney, Coriander Garlic, 102
Chutney, Instant Mango, 102
Chutney, Mint and Coriander, 102
Chutney, Yogurt Mint, 102
Coriander Garlic Chutney, 102
Coriander, Mint Chutney, 102
Creamy Green Chilli Drummettes, 50

Crunchy Drumsticks, 51
Cumin Coriander Powder, 105
Curried Apple Chicken Wings, 52
Curry, Mums Chicken, 74
Dad's Chicken Chaat, 41
Dal's Hot and Sour Chicken Soup, 18
Degi Chicken Korma, 71
Dopiaza, Chicken, 67
Drummettes, Creamy Green Chilli, 50
Drummettes, Mango Balsamic, 54
Drummettes, Silky Almond, 55
Drumsticks, Crunchy, 51
Drumsticks, Tandoori, 57
Gamenight Chicken Pizza, 100
Garlic, Coriander Chutney, 102
Garlic, Spicy Chicken, 94
Ginger Chicken, 96
Green Chilli & Paneer Wings, 53
Handi Kebab, 44
Honey Spiced Chicken Skewers, 35
Instant Mango Chutney, 102
Jakeys Butter Chicken, 86
Jalfrezi, Chicken, 69
Jalfrezi, Tandoori, 80
Kebab, Handi, 44
Kebab, Pistachio Chicken, 31
Kebabs, BBQ Chicken Malai Boti, 29
Kebabs, Chapli, 28
Kebabs, Reshmi, 32
Kebabs, Seekh, 46
Kebabs, Tunday, 45
Ketchup, Spicy, 104
Koftas, Chicken in creamy rich sauce, 62
Kolhapuri Chicken, 78
Korma, Almond Chicken, 70
Korma, Chicken - British Style, 84
Korma, Chicken - Delhi Style, 63
Korma, Degi Chicken, 71
Korma, Malabar Chicken, 81, 82
Lahori Chicken & Chickpeas, 73
Legs, Tandoori Roast Chicken, 58
Malabar Chicken Korma, 81, 82
Manchurian, Chicken, 98
Mango Balsamic Drummettes, 54
Mango Chicken Salad, 19
Masala, Chicken, 104
Meatloaf, 93
Methi Chicken, 77
Mint and Coriander Chutney, 102
Mint, Yogurt Chutney, 102
Mulligatawny Soup, 15
Mums Chicken Curry, 74
Noodles, Chicken Hakka, 99
Pakora, Chicken, 39, 40
Papajis Butter Chicken, 85

Mindfully Spiced Chicken • Page 106

Pickle, Chicken, 103
Pistachio Chicken Kebab, 31
Pizza, Gamenight Chicken, 100
Pulao, Quick Chicken, 90
Pumpkin Chicken, 65
Quick Chicken Pulao, 90
Raj's Yogurt Chicken, 89
Reshmi Kebabs, 32
Salad, Arabic Chicken and Peach, 21
Salad, Mango Chicken, 19
Salad, Spiced Coronation Chicken, 20
Salad, Spiced Orange and Chicken, 22
Salad, Tikka, 24
Samosa, Chicken, 27
Seekh Kebabs, 46
Serena's Baked Chicken Strips, 34
Sesame, Sweet and Spicy Chicken, 95
Shashlik, Chicken, 43
Shwarma, Chicken, 33
Silky Almond Drummettes, 55
Skewers, Honey Spiced Chicken, 35
Soup, Chicken and Mushroom, 17
Soup, Chicken and Tomato, 16
Soup, Dal's Hot & Sour Chicken, 18
Soup, Mulligatawny, 15
Soup, Thai Coconut Chicken, 23
Spiced Coronation Chicken Salad, 20
Spiced Orange and Chicken Salad, 22
Spicy Garlic Chicken, 94
Spicy Ketchup, 104
Spicy Stilton Chicken Burgers, 94
Spicy Sweet Garlic Wings, 56
Spinach Chicken, 68
Strips, Serena's Baked Chicken, 34
Sweet and Spicy Sesame Chicken, 95
Tandoori Drumsticks, 57
Tandoori Jalfrezi, 80
Tandoori Roast Chicken Legs, 58
Thai Coconut Chicken Soup, 23
Tikka Masala, Chicken - British Style, 72
Tikka, Chicken Boti, 30
Tikka, Chicken Turnovers, 36
Tikka, Salad, 24
Tunday Kebabs, 45
Turnovers, Chicken Tikka, 36
Vindaloo, Chicken, 83
Wings, Black Pepper & Cumin, 48
Wings, Cajun Mango, 49
Wings, Curried Apple Chicken, 52
Wings, Green Chilli & Paneer, 53
Wings, Spicy Sweet Garlic, 56
Yogurt Mint Chutney, 104

Printed in Great Britain
by Amazon.co.uk, Ltd.,
Marston Gate.